Nobody Told Me That!

Nobody Told Me That!

10 Tools for Parenting Happy, Healthy Children

RONI JAY

Vice President, Publisher: Tim Moore
Associate Publisher and Director of Marketing: Amy Neidlinger
Acquisitions Editor: Jennifer Simon
Editorial Assistant: Pamela Boland
Development Editor: Russ Hall
Operations Manager: Gina Kanouse
Digital Marketing Manager: Julie Phifer
Publicity Manager: Laura Czaja
Assistant Marketing Manager: Megan Colvin
Cover Designer: Alan Clements
Managing Editor: Kristy Hart
Project Editor: Anne Goebel
Copy Editor: Paula Lowell
Proofreader: Kathy Ruiz
Indexer: Cheryl Lenser
Compositor: Gloria Schurick
Manufacturing Buyer: Dan Uhrig

© 2009 by Pearson Education, Inc.
Publishing as FT Press
Upper Saddle River, New Jersey 07458

FT Press offers excellent discounts on this book when ordered in quantity for bulk purchases or special sales. For more information, please contact U.S. Corporate and Government Sales, 1-800-382-3419, corpsales@pearsontechgroup.com. For sales outside the U.S., please contact International Sales at international@pearson.com.

Company and product names mentioned herein are the trademarks or registered trademarks of their respective owners.

Printed in the United States of America

First Printing March 2009

ISBN-10: 0-13-815673-5
ISBN-13: 978-0-13-815673-2

Pearson Education LTD.
Pearson Education Australia PTY, Limited.
Pearson Education Singapore, Pte. Ltd.
Pearson Education North Asia, Ltd.
Pearson Education Canada, Ltd.
Pearson Educación de Mexico, S.A. de C.V.
Pearson Education—Japan
Pearson Education Malaysia, Pte. Ltd.

Library of Congress Cataloging-in-Publication Data
Jay, Roni.
  Nobody told me that!: 10 tools for parenting a happy, healthy children / Roni Jay.
    p. cm.
  Includes index.
  ISBN-10: 0-13-815673-5 (pbk. : alk. paper)
  ISBN-13: 978-0-13-815673-2 (pbk. : alk. paper) 1. Child rearing. I. Title.
HQ769.J376 2009
649'.7—dc22

                                   2008043367

Table of Contents

Contents

Contents

Contents

About the Author

Roni Jay is a mother of three young children and step-mother to three more (now grown up). In trying to be the very best parent she could be, Roni has studied what exactly it is that the most skilled parents do, and from this observation and her own personal experience as a front-line mom, distilled the 10 Tools for Parenting Happy, Healthy Children.

Roni is widely admired by everyone who knows her as a very talented, instinctive parent, who shows endless skill in handling children of very different personalities, and knowing just the right thing to say and do in every situation. There are many grateful parents today who are using Roni's clever tactics with their own children.

Roni's drive to write this book was the fact that although parenting is a very tough job, most books for parents are focused on the baby and toddler years, and very little is written to support and inspire parents of children from toddlers upward.

Introduction

It's often said that the most important thing you can do for your children is to love them. Well, yes, of course it is. I'm taking it as obvious that you love your kids, and you don't need any book to help you do that. But, whatever anyone says, love is not enough. So, what else really matters?

We do a million and one things for our children, from teaching them to walk, through checking to ensure they have clean socks, to making sure they know how to stay safe, and we listen to them tell us for the fifth time how they scored the winning goal in their playground game of basketball or football.

No parent has time to do everything (and nor would it be good for our kids if we did). That's even truer if you have more than one child, or a demanding job, or are on your own. So how do you decide what you absolutely must do and what you can let go? Unless you want to live in a permanent state of guilt, angst, or trepidation, spending some time thinking about what things will make the biggest difference to your child and what you can afford to let ride really makes sense.

Let's think about what you're aiming for. You want your kids to enjoy their childhoods, and you want them to grow into healthy, confident, successful adults who will be happy and will make those around them happy, too. Recognizing that goal starts to focus your mind—but how do you narrow it down further to the "must do" priorities? How do you know what's really, really important?

I've spent many years watching lots of children grow up, with great fascination. Not to mention my own—I have three children, and three stepchildren whose lives I became involved with in their early teens. This deep fascination with what parents do and the effect these actions have on their children has also led me to ask many adults about their own childhoods. When I pulled all this information together, the picture that emerged clearly indicated that parental input makes the most difference.

I've narrowed down the real essentials to 10 broad principles. These are the things that you need to get right in order to set your children up for the best possible life. You can get them right in your own way, of course—we're all different. Occasionally, I should warn you, you'll get them wrong. We all do that. You'll realize you got it wrong and you'll make amends, so that will be okay, too. After all, your children don't need perfect parents (how excruciating would that be?).

Your children need parents who put them first. I'm guessing that you put your children above yourself in your priority list. That's good; that's one similarity I've noticed among all the best parents I know.

There's a lot of very important stuff in this book that will make a big difference to your children—but don't panic. I bet you're doing a lot of it already, and the fact that you're reading this book shows you take your job as a parent seriously, which is a big plus. Assuming you're human, however, there are bound to be some important things that you haven't thought through.

We tend to have certain principles we feel are important (often having to do with what influenced our own childhoods) and others that we don't really think about. This book can help you spot the gaps so that you can give attention to the most important things you could be doing for your children.

Doing some of these things may be hard work; some of them will come naturally. Irritatingly, some of the pieces you find difficult will come naturally to your partner, but that works both ways. On the plus side, however, working on the difficult pieces will help you realize just how much of what you do for your children isn't so important. Best of all, after you have these 10 bases covered, you can stop stressing about the rest, and get on with being a great parent and enjoying your child.

Make Their World Solid

Few things are more important than giving your children confidence and self-assurance. Those are qualities that will enable them to get the rest of what they need for themselves.

Self-confidence comes largely from being confident in the world around you. If you can trust your own world to be solid and unchanging (in the right ways) it's far easier to be sure of your own place and personality within it. Your job is to make sure that everything important in your children's world is consistent.

On top of that, you need to make sure they feel good about themselves. You need to tell them how kind they are, not how selfish they are. You need to remind them that being the fastest swimmer isn't as important as being a good loser. You need to show them that they can do more than they realize, and that you believe in them.

Set Clear Boundaries That Don't Move

Setting clear, unchanging boundaries is just about the most essential discipline skill of all. It is vital for your children that the rules never change and are always enforced. The more emotionally shaky your children are, the more they will push these boundaries, but the boundaries must never move. A child who is having a tantrum, or who is going through an unsettled time, tests the boundaries frequently, not because the child wants you to back down, but because the child wants to make sure the boundaries are still there—the one constant the child can depend on, the one solid thing in a shifting world.

Actually, the better you are at keeping the boundaries fixed, the easier it will be keeping your kids in line. After they know that you *never* give in, they'll stop bothering to ask. They don't want to waste their time. Not only will they feel happier and more confident, they'll also take no for an answer.

That means no more asking to stay up a little bit longer before bed, no more nagging you to buy this or that toy as you go around through stores with them, no more begging to get the back yard pool out when you simply don't have time for it today. No more asking for anything after you've said no.

How often have you heard other parents complain, "My children never do what I say. They just push and push until eventually I give in just to shut them up." These parents are making a rod for their own back. Why do the children push and push? Because they know if they carry on long enough their parent will cave in. It's really hard, if you've fallen into this trap, to climb back out of it—but it can be done. Doing so will be much harder for you than it is for parents who have never given in, and whose children never push that hard, because your kids will take a long time to learn that you really are never going to back down, and they might as well stop asking.

I can promise you that parents who always mean no when they say it, honestly do have children who don't push. Their children may complain, whine, and throw a tantrum—though less than they would otherwise—but they don't keep on asking for something they've been told they can't have.

If you are in the habit of giving in—maybe not often, but even once or twice is enough for your kids to think it's worth pushing—you need to keep reminding yourself that if you can just hold out long enough, eventually your children will turn into kids who don't push. You won't get your reward today or tomorrow or next week, but you'll get it in the end if you're firm enough, and boy will it be worth it when your kids finally give up, forever, trying to change your mind.

Use the Word "No" Wisely

I know a few parents who tend to start off by saying no to their children, and then decide they're being unfair and back down. I watched a mother do this in stages the other day. Her daughter asked to get some painting gear out on the kitchen table while I was there. Wanting to chat rather than supervise, she said, "No, but if you leave us alone to chat for half an hour I'll let you paint later." Her daughter kept nagging, and in the end the mother got fed up because it was impossible to have a conversation over the nagging. So she said, "Well, tell you what, you can just get the paints ready, but then you really must go and give us some peace and quiet for a few minutes or I won't let you paint." The little girl got out the paints and then started pestering her mother to help her get the paper out, and some water for the brushes, and the mother kept saying, "Well, alright, but then you must leave us alone." Of course, the child never left us alone, but when her mother's back was turned she gave me a thumbs up with a huge exaggerated smirk of triumph on her face.

The poor mother had backed herself into a corner. She started off saying no and then felt guilty because she was putting her desire for a bit of peace and quiet before her daughter's desire to do some painting. There are only two ways round this quandary:

➤ Follow through on what you say, including not allowing the child to paint later on if he or she keeps pestering you and put up with the guilt.
➤ Don't say no in the first place.

It's always wise to do a quick, thinking-on-your-feet review of the likely outcome before you say no to anything. If you can't do it quickly, tell your child, "I'll have to think about that," or, "Give me a minute," or that dreadful phrase, "We'll see...." I say dreadful because I hated it as a child, but I have to admit it's the best approach. I had a conversation about this phrase once with a friend who said she hated it because it always meant no. Oddly enough, with my parents, it almost always meant yes.

I'll tell you why it can be so useful to think twice before you say no to anything (though any child will hate me for this). Apart from the obvious—that if you haven't said no you can't feel pressured to back down—it also means you have time to think through all the ramifications and set conditions before agreeing. So you might end up telling your child the following:

> "You can do some painting as long as you get everything out for yourself."

> "You can play in the backyard pool, but if you make a fuss about getting out when it's time to stop, I won't get it out again tomorrow."

> "If you don't pester me at all while we are shopping, I'll get you a treat at the end" (which shouldn't be anything unhealthy in this instance—see Chapter 9, "Show Them That Broccoli Can Be Fun").

It's important that you stick to these threats if they don't hold up their part of the deal.

By setting clear boundaries, and enforcing them with utter consistency, and by making sure that no means no, your children will be able to grow confidently, knowing exactly where the invisible parameters of their world are, and trusting them to stay put.

Carrots Are Better Than Sticks

You want your child to feel good about herself and to be encouraged to behave well. Apart from anything else, a well-behaved child lives in an emotionally much safer, kinder, more solid world. I don't mean well-behaved as in reserved and goody-goody and speaking only when spoken to. I can't stand it when parents do that to their children. I mean children who squabble and get into minor scrapes here and there, but only because they didn't think things through, or kids who are well-meaning and prefer to make you happy, but who still shout too loudly from time to time, or forget to sit properly on their chair.

Unless your children live in very troubled circumstances, from family break-ups to conditions such as ADHD, it really shouldn't be a problem, with firm boundaries and all the other elements covered in this book, for them to be well-behaved. However, there will be times when they will struggle to meet your standards, and when that happens you need to motivate them to muster the behavior you need.

Maybe you need your child to be better at getting up for school in the mornings, or remembering to put clothes in the laundry basket, or to stop shrieking. There are countless ways you can motivate kids to do these things, but there is one basic rule:

CARROTS ARE BETTER THAN STICKS.

By that, I don't only mean that carrots are kinder and more loving than sticks (which they are), but also that they are more effective. Your children are far more likely to get up for school in the mornings if you promise them a bonus of some kind at the weekend if you have no trouble all week, than if you threaten them with a punishment should they fail.

So, always opt for rewards rather than threats when you want to modify your children's behavior. By focusing them on success rather than failure, you're more likely to get results. It's far more reassuring to grow up with parents who want to reward you for being good than parents who want to punish you for being bad.

6

Rewards Versus Bribery

Let me clarify the difference between rewards and bribery, because it's relevant here. If your children are in the middle of doing something they know they shouldn't, and aren't stopping when you tell them to, it is bribery to offer them a reward for getting off the swing or abandoning the tantrum.

However, if they are currently behaving perfectly well or the problem behavior isn't naughty but simply forgetfulness (such as not putting their clothes in the laundry basket), offering them a reward is a legitimate incentive. This applies to getting out of bed for school: If while trying to get them up and out of bed at 7 a.m. you offer them a reward to get out of bed, that's bribery. But if, when they go to bed on Sunday, you offer them a reward if they give you no trouble right through to next weekend, that's a valid incentive.

Sticks and Carrot Sticks

There is a place for sticks as well, mind you. Sometimes a carrot needs a stick lurking behind it, just in case the carrot isn't tasty enough:

> "If you can get up for school without trouble all week, I'll let you stay up to watch your favorite TV program on Saturday evening. If you don't, however, I'll have to assume the problem is that you're too tired, so your bedtime will be a half an hour earlier."

Try to lead with the carrot, though, and only introduce the stick if you can't achieve what you want without it.

There's another trick you can keep up your sleeve, too, and that's the carrot/stick. Sometimes your instincts tell you that

7

you want to use a carrot rather than a stick, but you don't want to reward your children for behavior that you feel is the least you can ask. For example,

> ➤ Your want to give your children an incentive to admit to having done something wrong.
> ➤ You want to encourage your children into some kind of behavior you feel they shouldn't need asking to do, such as turning off the TV when they stop watching.

In this case, you think of a stick, and then present it as a carrot by turning it around. So, for example,

> ➤ Instead of telling them, "If you don't tell me the truth, I won't give you your allowance," you tell them, "If you to lie to me I'll have to keep your allowance. If you're honest and you tell me the truth I won't do that." Of course, you may still have to punish them for the original offense; that depends on what it was.
> ➤ Instead of saying, "If you don't turn off the TV, I won't let you watch it for a week," you say, "The only solution I can think of is for you to stop watching the TV. But I'll give you one more week and if you remember to turn it off every time you stop watching, I won't have to do that."

Praise Beats Criticism

Just as carrots are better than sticks, so is praise better than criticism. Few things will make your children feel happier and more loved than the approval and recognition of their parents. Having talked about rewards earlier, it's worth remembering that very often all the reward your children need is for you to notice their achievement. That's true not only of little children but of teenagers, and even adults.

So make sure that you notice when your children have done well, and that you say so. Whether it's something small such as finally holding their fork correctly, or something big, such as coping well in a crisis, or getting the test result they worked so hard for.

You should praise your kids every day, probably several times, though mostly only in a small way. Praising the big achievements won't mean so much if you go overboard over every little thing. You'll have left yourself nowhere to go when you want to lavish praise on them. But, on daily basis, you can come out with plenty of little words of praise, such as

> "Thanks for getting ready so quickly."
> "I like the way you've drawn that pony's mane."
> "It's great to come downstairs to breakfast and find the places at the table already set."

You see, praise doesn't have to mean saying, "Well done!" although that can be part of it. Praise is anything that makes your child feel that she has done well and you noticed.

It's really important to praise your child for anything he's improved at, even if his standard is now no better than average. He absolutely needs to know, if you've been preaching to him

9

for months about something, that you've noticed he has stopped doing it. So make sure you say, for example,

> "By the way, you've been much better at getting up in the mornings the last week or two. Well done."

> "I've noticed that you hung the towels up after your shower the last few days instead of leaving them on the floor. Thank you."

> "It is nice not having to hurry you up. Well done for being ready on time."

Be Careful What You Praise Them For

Now, choosing what to praise kids for is hugely important, and it can be interesting to watch other parents sneakily and notice how they handle this. One of the strongest ways we pass on our values to our children is by our choice of what we praise them for. If you want your children to grow up to be confident, you need to be careful what you give praise for, and how effusive that praise is.

Suppose you only ever praise your children for school work when they do well in exams and tests: "You had the best grade in the class? That's fantastic!" Or, "You only came in third? Well, never mind, that's still pretty good." If this is the only way they can get your approval, they'll grow up thinking that academic—and then career—achievement is the most important thing in life.

Then again, you could say to them, "You've worked so hard for these exams; that's the important thing, whatever grade you get." Or maybe, "You got a B? That's very respectable." Now you're telling them that it's good to work hard but it's not a huge deal beyond that how high up the class you come.

You'll have noticed here that you can't help but send out some kind of message by your response. But what else are you praising them for? If this is it, that's a very strong message. More likely, though, you praise them for other things, too. Perhaps you tend to dismiss good exam results in favor of telling them the following:

> "That was a really kind thing to do, giving your Matchbox car to Fred."
>
> "You're such a help in the mornings, I don't know how I'd manage without you."
>
> "I'm impressed by how brave you were, climbing right to the top of that ladder."

You might look at that list and think how much better to be praising your child for good character traits rather than achievement. Well, maybe, but you could still expand on this list. How about

> "I know you're not a morning person, so I'm pleased that you managed to put the milk and cereal on the table."
>
> "I know you don't like heights, so you did very well to get halfway up the ladder. I thought you were very brave for trying."

Aha! Now we're praising not only for achievement but for effort. Better still. In fact, you should be praising your children—in the sense of letting them know that you noticed—for a wide range of skills, talents, personal attributes, achievements, efforts, and all the rest of it. Just monitor yourself and make sure you aren't sending out messages you don't really want to send. If you always praise more for sporting than academic achievement, or more for effort than success, you're sending your child a very strong message.

This is especially important if you have more than one child. Giving more weight to, say, academic than sporting successes might work for your bright, non-sporty child. But what will the effect be on his brother or sister who is great at sports, but struggles a bit with schoolwork?

Praise Can Mean Pressure

Here's another thing. Your children really want you to acknowledge their achievements. If they can get noticed only by getting As on tests, they'll feel huge pressure to do so. If you only praise them for being kind and thoughtful, they'll be frustrated by the fact that you never seem to notice all the hard work they put in at school.

> You need to make sure that you are recognizing your children's achievements in everything that matters to them, regardless of how high up your priority list it comes.

There's another way, too, that you can put pressure on your children by the way that you praise them, and that's if you praise them out of proportion to their achievements. If they're talented in art and you keep telling them they're the next Picasso, they'll feel they have to keep achieving to keep earning your praise. Only they can't keep achieving, because actually they're not the next Picasso at all. So don't tell your eleven-year-old that he's a genius for learning to tie a tie. Just tell him well done. Don't tell your two-year-old how incredibly clever she is when she's just quite bright. Simply tell her,

"You're a smart cookie," or praise the action rather than the whole person by saying, "That was clever, solving that math problem."

How to Make Them Really Glow

If you want to give your children the best possible feeling, be specific about what you're praising, and ask them questions about it. I'm not suggesting you do this for every tiny thing, but when something is important to them it will make them feel you're really interested (which you are). For example,

> "I like the way you've drawn that horse's mane. It really looks as if it's flying in the wind. How did you get it to do that?"

> "Your swimming is so much better than the last time I took you. I can't believe how your breast-stroke has improved since you've been swimming at school. How many lengths can you do now?"

Praise Them, and Criticize Their Behavior

Though you might like to be able to praise your children all the time, there will inevitably be occasions when their behavior isn't up to scratch and you have to proffer some kind of criticism. This is not something to do carelessly, as in "Your handwriting really is awful," or, "You're hopeless at getting up in the mornings," or, "You're so irritating."

Aim never to speak negatively to your child without thinking it through first. When you do have to do it (as indeed you do from time to time), don't criticize them personally; criticize their skill or behavior:

> "That handwriting of yours could be a bit neater, don't you think?"
> "You were almost late for school this morning."
> "That high-pitched yell is really irritating."

If you attach the negative label to your children personally, they are much more likely to try and live up to it. "I might as well not bother. I'm just lazy so why make the effort?" Or, "Of course I shout a lot. I'm a noisy person." As you can see, this label can undermine their confidence and make them feel bad about themselves, which is the opposite of what you want.

So make criticism

> ➤ **Specific**—Let them know exactly what it is you want them to address. Not, "You're selfish," but, "It's selfish not to share toys. I'd like you to let your little brother play with that for a bit."

14

➤ **Constructive**—Let them see how this can be made positive. Not, "Your handwriting is just awful," but, "You know, with just a little bit of practice, your writing could be so much neater."

➤ **Solvable**—Don't criticize anything your child can't change: "You're hopeless at spelling," or, "You'll never become a football player."

Make Sure They Know Their Strengths

For your children to be really confident and grounded, they need to know what they're good at. We're not talking about being arrogant; to be honest, that usually comes from insecurity rather than over-confidence. Besides, arrogance doesn't hurt anyone else, and their friends will soon knock it out of them, so don't worry about that. Telling your children they're good at a sport doesn't make them arrogant—to do that, you have to imply that being good at sports makes them better in some way than people who aren't good at sports.

No doubt you know pretty much what your children's strengths are, and you'll help them by telling them as much:

"You really are a good diplomat. There seem to be fewer squabbles when you're around."

"Do you know, I wish I'd had half your ability at math when I was in school."

"Could you help me organize the toy cupboard? You're so good at working out where things should go."

There are, however, a few things you have to look out for when showing your children where their strengths lie:

- ➤ As with praise, make sure you let them know that strengths can come in lots of different shapes and sizes, from positive characteristics like kindness and bravery, to academic skills, art, sport, music, and other traits such as tidiness, a sense of humor, or good organizational ability. Don't focus on one type of strength to the exclusion of others.

- ➤ Try not to miss any of your children's strengths, or to be aware of them but miss telling your children. Your never mentioning a strength they feel they have may undermine their confidence.

- ➤ Don't forget that children change. You may have it stuck in your head that your child is dreadful at keeping track of time, but, in fact, he may have become really good at it over the last few months. It's amazing how long it can take to notice this sort of transformation.

- ➤ This next point ties in closely with how you praise children: Make sure you don't imply that certain strengths have more inherent value than others. This is especially true when you have more than one child. If you set more store by, say, your daughter's thoughtfulness than you do by your son's self-discipline, you will undermine your son.

Give Them Challenges You Know They Can Meet (and They Don't)

A great way to boost your child's self-esteem and confidence is to keep stretching them, in whatever field you know they're good at. Ask them to achieve something that you know will surprise them. For example, ask your 10-year-old to cook dinner for the family (it's fine if it's just pasta with a simple sauce). If she's never done this before, she'll feel so proud of herself, and suddenly believe she has the ability to be a good cook.

You can certainly set your children challenges in competitive areas, such as sport or academic work, but make sure they can achieve it, and don't set them up to compete directly with other people. Rather than suggest they try to get an A in English, maybe challenge them to get the best grades possible by the end of term.

Let Them Know They're Special

Your children need to know that they are special both to you and in themselves. They won't have certain strengths their siblings have, or not to the same degree, but they have others instead. Remind them (if you have more than one child) that if all children were the same there would be no point in having more than one. It's their unique differences for which you love them.

Tell your children that it simply doesn't matter if they're not as strong, or brave, or clever, or musical as someone else. Your children have other strengths—go on, tell them what they are—that make them stand out from the crowd.

17

This is especially important if your child has any kind of inherent disadvantage, such as a physical affliction, or a behavioral condition, that means that he struggles more than most children in some areas. If your child has Asperger's syndrome, remind him that people such as Michelangelo and Einstein are thought to have had that condition, too. If he's dyslexic, point out that it never did Muhammad Ali or Agatha Christie any harm—or Einstein. If your child is physically disabled, tell him how special people like Stephen Hawking and Christopher Reeve and Stevie Wonder have dealt with it. Your child has plenty of strengths regardless of the disadvantages he has, or perhaps is even stronger because of them.

The other situation where it is especially important to make sure your children know they are special is if you have twins, triplets, or more. They are, unfortunately, likely to encounter more trying circumstances than other siblings when they get lumped together and apparently treated as clones, especially if they are the same sex. This can be complicated by the fact that they may well, superficially, want to be like each other. It's all very well telling parents of same-sex twins that they shouldn't dress their children alike, for example, but that disregards the fact that their children may want to wear what their twin is wearing.

You can help things along a bit, for example, by not buying two of any item of clothing so that, while they can both choose to wear a pink T-shirt, they won't be identical. You can resist all temptation to refer to them as "the twins." On top of that, you can help enormously by letting each of them know their own strengths and how they should feel individually special. After all, *you* don't need to be told that your children are as different as any other two siblings. Just make sure that they know it from the start and they'll be far better equipped to ignore any suggestions to the contrary from misguided teachers, relatives, or friends.

Remind Them That You Are Not Perfect Either

If your children are unsure of themselves because they know they lack certain strengths, one of the most reassuring things you can do—as well as pointing out where they are particularly able—is to remind them that even you are not perfect. This may come as news to a young child (no, it won't be news to your teenager). Discovering that you've never been much good at music either, or that your mother was driven mad by your outbursts of temper, could be a revelation. If their revered mother or father has gotten through life despite being tone deaf, or having a short fuse, then clearly it is possible to overcome these drawbacks and live a normal life after all.

Your Relationship with Your Spouse

Now here's a tricky topic for some parents. Your children's world will not be as solid as you'd like unless they can see that your relationship is solid—and especially solid where it concerns them. This is one of the few areas of parenting that is significantly easier for single parents, though it will come back into play if you get involved in a new relationship with someone who is around enough to take on a parenting role with your children.

It is essential that your children feel safe and secure, and they can't do that in a household where tempers are volatile. You owe it to the children to make sure that you sort out differences so that the children don't get caught in the firing line or feel they must tread on eggshells.

Don't Argue in Front of the Kids

Not arguing in front of the kids doesn't mean you can't ever argue. It is far better for children to grow up with parents who rarely argue than parents who do all the time. But, actually, it's not ideal to have parents who never argue. How are you supposed to learn how to handle conflict if you never see it? How will you know that couples can argue and it's okay—they still love each other and make up afterwards?

The best scenario is for children to see that arguments are rare but can happen from time to time. When they do, their parents get angry with each other but never violent, and they don't say terrible things that everyone regrets forever. They make their feelings clear, but they do their best to be rational and to find a resolution to their argument. When they have resolved it, they're affectionate and loving and the air is clear.

This scenario teaches children everything they need to know:

> ➤ Most problems can be resolved without arguments.
> ➤ Occasionally, people do argue.
> ➤ It's okay to say how you feel.
> ➤ It's not okay to be violent or abusive.
> ➤ You should stay in control of your emotions so you can reach a solution.
> ➤ Just because people argue it doesn't mean they stop loving each other.

Present a United Front

There are, of course, plenty of subjects you shouldn't argue about in front of the children, ranging from whether you can stand another weekend with the in-laws, to whether or not you should try that thing with the handcuffs again after the kids are asleep. But the absolutely most important thing you should never ever argue about in the children's earshot is the children themselves.

If you disagree about how to treat the children, discuss it when either you or they are out of the house. Suppose you think it's essential they be fed a really healthy diet, and are furious because you came home today to find your fellow parent feeding the children fish sticks and French fries. Or maybe you think the children should be made to do their homework no matter how much they complain, while the other parent thinks they should be allowed to leave it and pay the consequences at school.

The vital rule to grasp here—unless your partner is advocating locking the kids in a closet for hours at a time, or something similarly abusive—is that it matters far more that the two of you present a united front, than whether your children eat fish sticks or fail their homework assignments.

For your children to be confident and to have a solid world around them, they need parents who agree on the way to bring them up. It's fine if mom puts up with a bit more whining than dad, or if dad lets them climb a higher tree when they go to the park. If only one parent is there, and as long as the key behavior rules don't change, it's okay for these minor things to vary. The important thing is that mom and dad are both in agreement that she puts up with more whining and he lets them climb bigger trees.

21

You will seriously undermine your children's confidence if you tell them that you disagree with what your partner does (and I'm afraid this is even more true if you're separated or divorced and the partner in question is an ex). When your child says to you, "But Mom always lets us have chocolate when we go shopping," the correct response is not, "Well I think she's irresponsible." If you're not happy about it, you can simply say, "Fine, but I don't." Then, if you feel strongly about it, raise the matter with your partner later. (I'd like to say in her defense that if she doesn't buy chocolate for the kids, she won't be able to buy it for herself...I can see where she's coming from here.)

So, when you find your partner doing something that horrifies you, don't launch into a heated debate. Wait until you're alone and then broach the subject. Don't forget, it's your relationship that is the most important thing of all to your children's confidence.

A Solid Foundation

Some children will always be more self-assured than others, and will grow into more confident adults. However, if you make sure your children's world is solid and they feel good about themselves, you'll create children whose confidence is at least sufficient that it won't hold them back. In the vast majority of cases you'll turn out a young adult who is happy to face the world and can cope comfortably with all the challenges of being a grown-up. You just need confidence in yourself that you can do it.

Give Them Some Magic

Many years ago, before I had children of my own, I visited a friend who had two boys about six and eight. The boys asked me if I would like to meet their flying cat. I said I would be delighted, and they introduced me to a rather charming black-and-white cat that was dozing under a bush. I remarked that it didn't seem to be flying at the moment. No, they explained, it never flew when anyone was looking. I asked how they had ever found out, in that case, that it could fly, and they said that they had never seen it themselves but they just knew.

I've always remembered this because I had a disappointing number of friends who were in the habit of telling their children things like, "Cats can't fly" or "Dragons aren't real, you know."

When you're very small, anything is possible. The moon *is* actually looking at you, you could grow up to be a superhero, and your cat might really fly. As you get older, slowly the world starts to anchor into place around you. Your perception becomes fixed, and fixed into the same boring rut as everyone else's. The moon can't actually see, you can't develop superpowers, and, obviously, your cat can't fly. It's sad, really.

As your world gets weighed down, so does your imagination. It all gets boxed in—along with your creativity and your ability to think laterally. So why inflict that on our kids sooner than we have to? I was impressed with my friends who had resisted the temptation to cast doubt on their amazing flying cat's abilities (the parents knew all about it), because that's what children need: They need the magic to last as long as possible.

I've never understood how so many parents join in the Santa Claus conspiracy (well, you have to, or you would be ostracized by all the other parents at school) but don't provide their children with any other magic. Yet, magic is what childhood is all about—freedom from tedious reality, freedom from responsibility, freedom from the constraints of adult life. Over the 18 years we have to raise our children, we have to slowly feed them reality, responsibility, and obligations, but we should be fighting to keep the magic alive as long as we can.

Give Them Space

The first and most basic requirement children need to enjoy the magic is a blank canvas. They can do magic all by themselves, they just need us to get out of the way. Small children can believe in all sorts of things we can't. Their bedroom floor really is a miniature battlefield, the backyard kiddie pool becomes an Olympic pool, and those Legos *are* really a spaceship.

What's more, children are free of the forethoughts that can ruin things for us. When I was about 18, I laid on a beach and let the waves wash round me. As much as I enjoyed the sensation, I couldn't entirely shake off the thought of what a pain it was going to be to wash all the sand out of my long hair. (I didn't know the half of it—it took hours.) Small children can get blissfully covered in mud or paint without a thought about all the cleanup they'll have to go through to get it all off—as long as we keep our mouths shut and don't spoil it for them by pointing it out.

Clear Some Time for Them

The biggest inhibitor for many children is that they just don't have enough time to do magic. They are carted from ballet to soccer practice to clarinet lessons to drama—and dragged around to half their brother's or sister's events, too. Now, as lovely as it is to participate in ballet or drama, it's not more important than doing nothing at all, which is pretty important itself.

It's a good rule of thumb that when your children are elementary school age they generally shouldn't be doing more than two weekly, organized, out-of-school activities. If they're football mad, maybe both activities are football. If they want to take up something new, they should drop something else to do it. This system works very well for lots of children who really enjoy taking gymnastics or tae kwon do for a year or so, but have no desire to do it forever.

If they don't want to do a particular activity, they should certainly drop it—there's no merit in making your child learn the piano or be a boy scout or whatever it is. That's all about what *you* want, and their childhood should be about what *they* want. Sure, children should keep going until the end of the season after they're committed, or stick with drama until after the production so as not to let down the friends they're performing with, but then they should be allowed to stop.

The only exception I can really think of to this is swimming. This is a skill that could save their lives, especially if you live near open water, and it is useful when they're young to take them swimming once a week until they reach a certain standard. Try to make swimming one of the two activity sessions a week, and the faster they learn it the sooner they can drop it.

As your children get older, they will go to bed later, which frees up a bit more time. I'd never actively encourage them to do more than two extra activities a week, but if they're really eager there is scope to be more flexible after they get into late elementary school age and beyond.

I should also add that there is a very rare type of child who needs to be constantly stimulated and finds it hard to play imaginatively. Don't convince yourself you have this kind of child in order to justify dragging him off to three or four classes a week, because you probably don't have this kind of child. But they do exist, and they probably want to choose some quite quirky activities (these aren't the ballet/football type of kids). If you really truly have one of these children, you could consider giving him more like three or four activities a week.

Find Them an Empty Space

The less you do for them, the more your children's minds will do for themselves. So, rather than take children to an adventure park, a bowling alley, or a china-painting workshop, take them somewhere almost empty. That's not to say you should never take them to a street festival or the movies, because it's important that they have a wide range of experience, and these things can feed their imaginations later, but never forget that the real magic is in wide beaches and open hills and woods. What your children will find there is real magic, and they'll be free to create on their own.

Even if you live in the middle of a city, there are parks and open places that can stimulate your child. If you're taking them out for the day, why not hop on a train or a bus and head for open country? It needn't cost any more than the bowling alley or a movie and it's an adventure in the fullest sense of the word.

Best of all are the kind of open spaces where you can hide, or where the terrain is unusual. My children have spent literally hours in a quarter-acre site in Cornwall, which has the low walls of a 2,000-year-old Celtic village still in place. Sand dunes are another perfect landscape for creating games. Even the back garden—maybe with a few empty cardboard boxes supplied to kick-start their imagination—will give them hours of fun.

Equip them so you don't have to keep restraining them—so if you're worried about them getting soaked or muddy, then deck them out in head-to-toe waterproof clothes.

27

Be warned that if your children aren't used to entertaining themselves, they might need a little time to get into the idea or need ideas from you to get them started.

Computers and TV Kill Magic

Not only do screens of any kind, including PlayStations and Xboxes and all the rest, eat time, they also destroy magic. It's a scary thing, but if your children spend too much time in front of a screen, they will forget how to play. Honestly, I've seen it happen. There's more about this topic in Chapter 9, "Show Them That Broccoli Can Be Fun," in relation to their physical health, but too much screen time affects their ability to entertain themselves, too. So ration the time your children spend in front of a screen. Up until the early teenage years, two hours a day is plenty, with perhaps a little extra on non-school days when their two hours has been used up by breakfast time.

When your children become teenagers, you'll struggle to drag them away from their screens. As long as you don't allow computers or TV in their bedrooms, you should be fine. The groundwork has been laid by this time. My experience is that kids who spend all their time in front of a screen grow into adults who do the same thing. Kids who have limited screen time until early teens may pig out on TV and computers for a few years, but in time they revert and become adults for whom TV is an occasional pleasure rather than an essential way of life.

Magical Times

Your children will put a lot of the magic into their lives by themselves if you just give them the space and the freedom to do it— but you can still contribute in all sorts of ways.

Do you remember Christmas as a child? If you were lucky enough to have parents who made an effort, Christmas will have been that clichéd magical occasion that you see in books and films everywhere. That's what your child needs and you can have a lot of fun giving it to them. It's not silly, it's crucial to your child's development. It's those safe, secure, loving times that will create a child with the confidence and the self-assurance to cope in the big scary world when the time comes.

So, come on, what could you do to make Christmas even more magical? How about sprinkling glitter in front of the fireplace and putting Santa Claus bootprints in it for them to find on Christmas morning? Or how about hiding one present each and getting them to hunt for it? Or lighting the house only with candlelight after dusk on Christmas Eve? Why not all of those, and more? In fact, why not get your children to use those magical imaginations of theirs to come up with even more ideas?

After you get Christmas sorted out, what about Easter egg hunts? A bonfire night? Halloween? What about birthday parties with homemade cakes? Summer camping trips, and winter walks with flasks of cocoa? All of you snuggling up on the sofa under one blanket when the wind is howling and watching a favorite DVD as a treat? That's it, now we're starting to rock! These traditions aren't just an extra effort that no one appreciates. Even if the children don't tell you now that it matters to them, it really does.

Make It a Tradition

The best things of all for children are the routine activities that they repeat every year, or even more often. It's like asking for the same bedtime story night after night when they already know it by heart. Sometimes it seems pointless, but actually the fact they know it so well is the whole point. It makes it safe and predictable and secure, like a favorite stuffed animal or eating your favorite comfort food when you feel down (probably the thing your mother or father used to give you as a child). The whole point is that you always hide the biggest Easter egg in the garden, or it's always touch and go whether the Christmas pudding will turn out, or you always get a cooked breakfast on your birthday, or Grandma and Grandpa always turn up on Christmas Eve.

Pick Your Moment

I do realize that you have a life. You can't spend your entire time carefully hiding Easter eggs and such. Not with the shopping to do, the laundry, and a presentation to prepare for Monday's meeting. However, I don't think I know any family that makes a big deal out of absolutely everything. Some don't really do Easter, especially if they're non-Christian and only really interested in the candy eggs, but maybe they have a big birthday party for the children. Not many people make a big thing of both Easter and Palm Sunday, for instance.

The best way to make these things magical and memorable for your children is to put a huge effort into two or three big events every year, rather than do all of them half-heartedly. So, unless you have time for everything, just pick the ones you know matter most to your kids and think about how you can make them even more special. If you have two or more children, it can be more fun to have one huge, magical party a year rather than two or three little ones. They can have a few friends for a trip to a movie and a sleepover on their birthday, and then go all out with a huge combination party once a year.

Bedtime

It's worth singling out bedtime as being probably the best of all opportunities for everyday magic, at least up to the age when your kids insist on going to bed on their own.

A really good bedtime routine will give your child a feeling of magic, comfort, and security. They'll spend the rest of their lives trying to recapture it.

Ideally, start with a bath. It's a great way to relax, and cleaning children is, broadly speaking, a good thing anyway. After your children are clean and dry, you can head off to the bedroom. Snuggle them into bed, or sit them on your lap wrapped in a fleece blanket (baby blankets are worth keeping for this long after they've outgrown the crib). Read them a story or two, depending on how long the story is and how many children there are—maybe they choose one each. You can't beat the feeling of being snuggled up in your mother's or father's arms and listening to a story.

Finally, after you've read them the story, have a few special goodnight words that you always say. This not only reinforces their security, but also signals that you're going now. For example, when my children were little my husband always used to say, "You're the apple of my eye, the treasure of my chest, and the love of my life. Night, night, sleep tight, don't let the bed bugs bite, see you in the morning light, not too early." The children referred to these as "magic words," and wouldn't go to sleep without them. In fact, my youngest children still want to hear them every night. If they wake in the small hours, they can usually be settled down again with an offer of "magic words" that seem instinctively to send them off to sleep.

Magical Settings

It's not only events that can bring magic into your children's lives. It's also their natural surroundings. When your children are old enough, get together and redecorate their bedroom. Even on a limited budget you can still create a jungle, or an underwater scene, or a pink and silver princess bedroom. This is exactly the kind of thing that helps your child to feel special and safe, and as they curl up each night in their pirate lair or their pony stable, they can imagine they're really in the thick of it. The lines between magic and reality are so much finer for your child than for you. It's so easy to give them the magic they crave, that it would be a sin not to.

Dens

For some reason, there are few things that children enjoy more than making dens. I remember doing it as a child, outdoors with branches and rugs, and indoors with blankets and furniture. Children can construct their dens with huge creativity, and they often become a bear's cave or a soldier's dugout, as well as a safe space your children can call their own.

You can create a tree house (if you're lucky enough to have a suitable tree) or a playhouse for your children that will get endless use, and you can give them the knowledge to build their own, perhaps more temporary, structures. Don't moan about the blankets getting covered in twigs—just find them a blanket you don't care about so much and let them have it.

Indoors, allow your children to fill up the corners of their bedrooms or playroom with bizarre arrangements of cushions and tablecloths and upside-down chairs. Okay, you may need them

33

to clean up eventually, but let them have a good play first, and maybe even leave them up for a few days as a treat around the holidays.

You could even rig up a permanent den around their bed, which is something that most children love. You could fabric paint some cheap calico curtains, or let them do it themselves, or dye a mosquito net pink, or find some old curtains. There are few lovelier things than being able to give your children fun, magic, love, and security all in one.

Get Out of the Way

After you've done the vital job of giving your children some magic, and some freedom to enjoy it, all you have to do now is let them get on with it. Sometimes that can be quite difficult, as the mess builds up, and you can see how long it will take them to get the paint out from under their fingernails. But there's no point doing all this great work if you're not going to let them enjoy it. Don't try to make them think like adults about boring grown-up things like cleaning. Give them playthings that you're prepared to see muddied or damaged and then watch your children cover them in mud and accidentally tear them. That's where cardboard boxes are so good—you're less likely to intervene and find yourself saying, "Ooh, be careful!"

If you don't want your children to get grass stains on their pants, don't stop them rolling in the grass—just give them a different pair of pants. Don't make them conscious of mess by telling them to change their clothes three times a day. When they say, "My T-shirt is muddy," just reply, "Who cares?" I know that many girls, and some boys, will go through a phase of wanting their clothes clean without your encouragement, but don't pander to it. Let them change if that's what they want, but don't give the impression that it makes any difference to you. Otherwise as they get older they'll find it harder to enjoy themselves because they will worry about whether they're getting muddy or wet.

Obviously if your child is really filthy you may not want them bringing it into the house. A grass stain won't come off when it's on the furniture (or probably off the pants either, but too late now), but mud may, so it's reasonable to get her to change out of clothes that are filthy. But don't make a big deal of it— "Aaargh! How did you get so filthy?"—just make light of it and say, "My gosh, you've been having fun. Let's just change those pants before you get mud all over the house."

More Magic

The things that add magic to your children's lives are the ones that give them space and freedom to exercise their own imaginations. They have quite enough things already that restrict their minds. When people say, "Childhood doesn't last as long as it used to," what they mean is, "The magic doesn't last as long as it used to." Here are some of the best things for helping your children to keep the magic for as long as possible:

- Bedtime stories
- Stories you make up yourself
- Empty cardboard boxes, sticks, bits of string, and other assorted objects that can be endlessly adapted
- Open spaces—woods, beaches, parks, hills
- Water—lakes, rivers, streams, the sea, or even just a sprinkler
- Old places—historical sites, memorials, and so on
- Myths and legends—old tales
- Surprises
- Trips to the theater
- Fantasy movies (but only good ones)
- Dressing up boxes with costumes for make believe and fantasy games
- Holidays and day trips
- Picnics (peanut butter-and-jelly sandwiches will do fine—the food doesn't have to be important)
- Exploring and little adventures

Hmmm, oddly enough, those are almost all things that were around when we were young, and when our parents and even our grandparents were young. It just goes to show that the modern world has a lot to offer, but it doesn't make childhood any more magical than it always was. More of the books have color illustrations, and the movie special effects have gotten better, but the basic activities are pretty much the same. Because it's parents who give their children the magic they need, and that never changes.

Show Them How to Separate Right from Wrong

We all make mistakes. We know we do, and we also know it's human and it's normal. Trouble is, we often don't like admitting it in front of our children. But it's important that our children can tell when they've made a mistake. They should know that it's mostly fine to make mistakes, but they also need to know the difference between right and wrong in every situation. They need to be able to make the morally right choice when it matters.

As you'll see in Chapter 4, "Teach Them to Think," you want them to think for themselves. But as a parent you want to underpin this by making sure that what they think for themselves isn't, "If I steal this chocolate bar no one will catch me," or, "I know my friend's in trouble but I'm busy and, if I don't help, someone else is bound to step in." You have 18 years to instill in them the values you believe are important, so that when they think for themselves, they do it on the foundations you've laid.

37

What Do You Think Is Right and Wrong?

You need to be pretty confident of your own values as a parent. When you were childless and free you could get away with blurring the boundaries from time to time and no one but you would know. Maybe you would decide not to point out to the shopkeeper that they had given you too much change, or to tell your troubled friend you never got his message when, actually, you just didn't have the energy for him at the time.

After you have kids, you're being watched most of the time. Whenever your children are watching you, you have to set the right example. There's no point telling kids, "Do what I say, not what I do." Apart from the hypocrisy of it, it simply doesn't work. It's not how children are wired. They *will* do as you do, regardless of what you say. So make sure you do as you would want them to do in the same circumstances.

Most of us are pretty clear on the big stuff. We know we don't want our children to grow up murdering, raping, and pillaging, and, odds are, we aren't going to be doing a lot of that in front of them anyway. It's the smaller things that determine whether our children grow up to be honorable and trustworthy, or a bit unreliable and occasionally close to the edge. It's all that stuff to do with telling the truth, not complaining behind people's backs, handing in lost property rather than pocketing it, offering our seat to someone older, remembering to say thank you, living up to promises, and so on. Those are the everyday things we have to get right so our children get them right. After all, if we don't do it, how can we expect them to?

Where Do You Draw the Guilt Line?

The fact is that we all set certain standards for ourselves. But very few of us are really whiter than white. Every so often we cross over into a gray area where we're not doing anything dreadful, but we've nudged the boundaries. We know we've done it because secretly we feel a little guilty. You know the sort of thing: You know you can get away without buying a ticket if you're getting off at the next stop (which is technically theft, but hey—they should check them). Or you turn up 10 minutes late for your dentist appointment (well, she kept you waiting 10 minutes last time). Or you're complaining about that mother from school (but boy, is she irritating).

You see, we make excuses to ourselves for these little misdemeanors and acts of rudeness, but we only make those excuses because deep down we know we need an excuse—because actually traveling without a ticket, or being inconsiderate or rude, isn't acceptable.

If you allow your behavior to slip into these gray areas in front of your children, they'll think this behavior is okay. It's tough, really tough, behaving impeccably in front of your children, and often no fun at all. It has to be done. Otherwise all your gray areas of behavior will be programmed into your child as being whiter than white. So, when they become adults and when they develop their own gray areas, they'll be pushing the boundaries even further than yours. That means your child will become an adult who doesn't even feel guilty when they keep people waiting, or don't give up their seat on the bus, or even steal a ride on a bus.

Why does it matter? So what if our children grow into adults who stop speaking to a friend over some petty matter, or let someone else give up a seat on the bus? Well, it matters for two reasons. First, because the more honorable your child is (to use an old-fashioned word) the more good friends she will have. Some people may think it's a laugh if their friends behave disrespectfully, but actually, when they're in trouble, they want a friend they know is utterly trustworthy and reliable. Second, it matters because people who always behave with respect and integrity have higher self-esteem, and that's definitely something we want for our children.

What Values?

Drawing up a comprehensive list of all the values you want your children to inherit is virtually impossible, but you know perfectly well what they are. Some of them (the not committing violent crimes stuff, for example) are so obvious it's really not a problem. If you care enough to be reading this book, you're not going to be ambivalent about this kind of thing.

> The values that matter, and the ones for which you need to make an effort, are all those things that you make yourself do even when you don't really feel like it or it's difficult, because you feel you should. You make your kids do them because they should, even when they don't want to.

Essentially, all these values are about putting other people before yourself. It's easy to be selfish—you won't need to teach your children that. The values that matter are about making an effort on behalf of someone else, whether it's a friend or a multinational corporation. That effort may entail finding the money to pay for the things you should, resisting the temptation to pocket lost property, or getting out of the house earlier so you don't keep people waiting. The point is that you're suppressing your selfish instincts for someone else's benefit.

Young children aren't capable of putting other people's welfare before their own. If they choose to do "the right thing" over their own desire, it's because they think they'll get into trouble if they don't. In other words, it's still inherently a selfish choice. By around middle to late grade school age, your children should have grasped the concept of putting other people first, and hopefully will be able to make their own value-based choices, at least sometimes. In other words, your eight-year-old might ask someone she doesn't really like to her party because she doesn't actually want to hurt that person's feelings.

Your job is to spend those early years demonstrating the right behaviors and choices, so that by the time your children are old enough they can start applying the values you want them to

41

when they make their own decisions. You need to keep reinforcing those values so that they make the choices you think they should more of the time.

How to Instill the Right Values

So, how are you going to instill these values in your children? Setting an example is vitally important, of course, but you can also make sure that you spell out what you believe in and why. Instead of saying, "I know you wanted me to read you another chapter but I don't have time," why not say (assuming it's true), "I know you wanted me to read to you but I promised your Grandma I'd phone her, and I can't break a promise."

Suppose one of your children says, "I don't want to go to Ollie's party. I hate football. Can't I say I'm doing something else?" Instead of agreeing, ask your child how he would feel if Ollie lied to him. Then help him find an alternative that doesn't involve lying to Ollie. It's much better to say to Ollie, "I wouldn't enjoy it because I hate football, but would you like to come and play at my house next weekend instead?"

Siblings provide an endless supply of opportunities to point out how it feels when someone lets you down, lies to you, "borrows" your things without asking, annexes your friends, and all the other petty sins that brothers and sisters commit. So if you have more than one child, make sure they all recognize the lesson for themselves—and reassure yourself with the thought that they're treating their friends far better than they treat each other.

Another way you can reinforce your values is by the way you praise your children. If you praise them for exhibiting the values you want to see, they are far more likely to repeat and reinforce them. So tell them, "I thought that was a really coura-geous thing to do, well done," or "I was really happy to see you including Alice in your games, even though she slows you down because she's younger."

Taking Responsibility

Children also learn a huge amount about values and rights and wrongs when you give them responsibilities. Whether it's feeding a goldfish, or having a friend stay over, children need to recognize that they have to give in order to get, and that being unselfish will ultimately bring them more friends and a greater sense of confidence and integrity.

Whenever your children ask for something extra, make sure they understand exactly what you expect of them in return for the responsibility, and what will happen if they don't deliver on their side of the bargain. So, for example:

> ➤ **Going out to play on their own**—Whether it's at the park or the gym, on a bike, with a friend, or with the dog, your child needs to understand that in order to retain the right to go out to play, you require certain undertakings in return. For example, he must be back by an agreed time, he must be with a friend at all times, he must turn off his iPod if they're cycling on the road—whatever conditions you feel are important. Children need to know what will happen if they don't do this: You'll ban them from taking bike rides or from going with certain friends, or maybe even withdraw the right to play on their own alto-gether until they're older.

43

➤ **Having a friend to stay over**—This should imply some level of responsibility on your child's part. What if her friend trashes her room? Refuses to go to sleep? Talks her into raiding the fridge in the middle of the night? By the age of about six, your child needs to take on some responsibility for maintaining order if she wants to be allowed a sleepover. One of my children has one friend he won't ask for a sleepover anymore because he doesn't want to have to clean up after him and he can't get him to stop making a mess. My child recognizes that he just doesn't have the necessary force of personality to get this particular friend to cooperate, but he manages fine with his other friends who are less disruptive.

➤ **Doing homework unsupervised**—Most children start off doing their reading or occasional homework at the kitchen table with you supervising. They end up doing it in their bedroom where you have no idea if it's even getting done at all. Now, arguably, by the time they're coming up to their SATs there's not a lot you can do. But when they first ask to do their homework in their room, maybe between the ages of about 7 and 11, what will you expect in return for this new responsibility? Should they show you the completed homework? Do they have to finish it before bedtime rather than string it out and end up going to sleep late? Will you let them just carry on in their own way as long as you don't get reports back from school saying there's a problem? Suppose the teacher starts reporting that homework isn't being done. Will your child have to come back to the kitchen table or show you the completed homework before bedtime?

➤ **Having a pet**—Clearly it's important to match the pet to the child. You can't expect a three-year-old to clean out the pony stall every day. So you need to establish exactly what you are asking: Is your child exercising the pet? Feeding and watering it? Cleaning up after it? Training it? Should he remember these things for himself or will you remind him? Children also need to know what you'll do if they don't stick to these responsibilities. Sell or give away the pet? This one needs thinking through, because—as your child needs to recognize—animals have a right to be looked after and you need to make sure they're well cared for. Some pets can be hard to find a new home for. If your child wants a snake or a giant millipede you can't assume that you'll be able to find a new home for it easily. Maybe the deal is that if you end up looking after it, your child won't be allowed another pet until he is older.

Make It Fair

The example of the pet illustrates an important point here. It's not fair to your child to give her responsibilities she isn't capable of meeting. It will undermine her confidence if she lets you down when she was trying not to. So it's better to take on some of the responsibility yourself and hand it over slowly. Maybe you'll help your five-year-old clean out the hamster cage as long as he helps, and by the time he's seven you'll expect him to do it if you remind him. By the age of, say, nine, you might expect your child to remember for him- or herself (don't worry, hamsters don't usually live that long anyway).

If you have more than one child, this means that they may not be taking on the same responsibilities at the same age. That's fine. Maybe Sam is really responsible about looking after pets, but hopeless at keeping friends under control. Tilly, meanwhile, may have all her friends under her thumb but never remembers to walk the dog. So don't impose the same rules on different children without first considering what their capabilities are. There's more on this topic in Chapter 5, "Let Them Lead You."

Talk It Through

Your children need to recognize consciously that they are being given a new responsibility, and that they have to keep their side of the deal. So whether you're letting them ride their bike home from school, or cook their own lunch, it's important to talk it through with them and set out clearly:

> ➤ **Exactly what you're agreeing to**—Can they take any route home from school they like? Are they allowed to use the blender?

> ➤ **What you expect in return from them**—They phone if there's a problem or they're going to be late; they clean up everything right after they've eaten.

> ➤ **What will happen if they don't deliver**—They'll have to go back to walking home; they'll only be allowed to cook if an adult is free to supervise.

It's no good imposing these conditions on your child, of course, unless you get his agreement. He may point out that phoning is a problem because you haven't yet allowed him a cell phone, or that she doesn't know how to wash the blender. You can negotiate on these points until you find a route that you're both happy with.

Giving your children responsibility is the way to let them practice all those values that you've been busy instilling in them. It gives them a reason to put other people (or even pets) first, and to consider how someone else feels, and how to achieve the things they want with integrity. Will you worry without a phone call from them? Will their pet go hungry? Are they prepared to work hard even when they don't feel like it tonight?

Of course, your child won't get it right every time. Do you? I certainly don't. When they fall short, you'll need to talk through with them why it happened, and make sure they understand why their behavior wasn't okay.

Getting It Right

The values you give your child may well be those you got from your parents. You may be passing them on, not only to your child, but also to your grandchildren and for generations beyond. That's a wonderful thought. Children with strong values that are reinforced by their parents are happier for it; they know where they stand and a lot of their decisions are made for them.

Teach Them to Think

I have a friend whose 18-year-old badly wanted a particular job. Trouble was, the job was in London and this teenager was terrified of going to London all alone. He had no idea how to get around in a strange city, how to travel on the subway, how to work out a fare system, or go about finding help if he got stuck. And why not? Because he had never learned to think properly for himself.

Sure, this teen could do some things for himself—most 18-year-olds can—and there was a self-confidence thing going on here, too (as you saw in Chapter 1, "Make Their World Solid"). That's completely normal at that age, but it would have been minimized if he had had all the thinking skills he needed. You see, at the heart of it, his was a logistical problem. He simply didn't know how to follow a subway map, how to work out how long it would take him to get from home to the office, or how to figure out how to get a big load of groceries home without a car. In the end he passed up the job.

Now, there's no reason why your 18-year-old should know how to read a subway map if she's never traveled on the subway. But she should certainly have the skills to look at a map of any kind and think, "I can work this out," rather than look at it and think, "I don't know where to start." And the difference is all up to you.

Thinking isn't only about being able to apply logical mental processes, though that's an important part of it. It's also about being able to formulate ideas and opinions, and make decisions for oneself. Good teachers can help with this skill, but the bulk of the job is up to us as parents. Certainly if our children reach 18 unable to think effectively, we've no one to blame but ourselves.

The ABCs of Thinking

One of the most important ways you can encourage your child to think is to get him reading. I don't just mean the mechanics of it—though, of course that's an essential basis—I mean get him to enjoy reading books. As children get older, they'll pick up more ideas from reading than from anything else apart from talking, so it's a vital step on the way to thinking for themselves.

Good books are a different way to introduce your child to the concept of right and wrong, and the fact that it's not always a black-and-white distinction. Stories will help your children to think imaginatively for themselves. As they get older, newspapers and magazines will show them the arguments on both sides of an issue, and provide the background information for them to start formulating their own opinions.

There are few better things you can do for your child than encourage a love of reading. This needs to start at a young age, and built up until they can read easily by themselves. If you've done the job properly, you won't need to do much after this point apart from make sure they have access to plenty of books. Here's how to get your child to grow up assuming that books and reading are an integral part of life:

➤ Start reading to your child by the time she is six months old (hopefully, if you're past that point, you'll have done this already). Just talk or read through a board book and point out some of the pictures.

➤ As children get older, give them board books they can handle themselves without doing too much damage. Read to them every night at bedtime, and during the day. Get them to point at things ("Where's the cat?"), and to turn the pages themselves.

➤ As they get a little bit older, they'll probably want you to read the same book over and over again. This can seem somewhat pointless from an adult per- spective, but to a child it's important. There's huge security in anything familiar, and your child isn't quite as sure as you are that the story is going to end the same way every time. He has to learn that.

➤ You can keep your child on her toes now by occa- sionally getting the story wrong and seeing if she corrects you, or pointing at the dog and saying, "There's the cat!" so she can show you you're wrong.

➤ Make up stories for your child as well. He'll espe- cially like this if you put him into the story, along with his favorite toy, best friend, or pet.

➤ Ask your child questions about the stories you read, both as you read and afterwards. "What do you think Raffi should do? Should he tell the witch where the cat is hiding?" This is all part of getting your child engaged and thinking for herself.

➤ As your child gets older and is able to read to himself, make sure he has a ready supply of books. These are not a luxury item or a treat, but a basic necessity. If you have more than one child, buying some books that you think will be read and re-read can be cost effective. If the budget is tight, the library is an obvious source of good reading material, along with secondhand bookstores and swaps with friends.

➤ Never try to make your child read a book she doesn't enjoy. If she can't get into it after a couple of chapters, let her give up; otherwise, reading becomes a tedious chore instead of a delight. Besides, I give up if I'm not enjoying a book after the first few chapters, don't you?

Don't Answer All Their Questions

Sometimes children can be lazy. If they know you can tell them the answer to their questions, why should they bother to find out for themselves? To be fair, it's only what we all do. But your children need to know how to find the answers for themselves.

Obviously you'll have to help out with questions such as, "When will dinner be ready?" and "Has anyone seen my green T-shirt?" But when it comes to problem solving children should be given the chance to figure it out for themselves, and for broader questions you need them to learn to look things up in books and on the Internet, or to work out who to ask. By the time your child is a teenager and planning a vacation with friends, she needs to be able to phone a local tourist office for advice, or to look up the local bicycle repair shop in the Yellow Pages.

They won't learn any of these skills if you keep doing these things for them. So when they are young, give them small pointers toward solving a problem rather than just solving it for them. As they get older, get them to search the Internet, or to use the phone book and ask their questions on the phone. Conversely, if you never answer a question but always make them go off and research it, they may just give up asking questions. So I'm not suggesting you never give them the answer. But from time to time you can encourage them to find the answer for themselves.

Even a small child can do this with your help. If your six-year-old asks you how many million years ago the dinosaurs died out, chances are you might well know the answer (if your child has been into dinosaurs for a while). But instead of just blurting it out, help her find a good book and look the answer up together.

> Get into the habit of not just leaping to your child's aid or solving all his problems and answering every question before he has time to reflect. Instead make it a habit to ask, "How do you think you could do that?" or "Is there a way we could find that out?" or even just "What do you think?"

Practical Thinking Skills

Practical thinking skills are another vital area your child needs to work on, beginning as soon as possible with learning how to use an index. He should be taught this at school sooner or later, but it's at home he'll get the best chance to practice it, and to see you using the skill yourself.

It's crucial that your child sees you practicing these skills, because that's what shows him that normal adult life will require him to be able to use a dictionary or read a map. And as soon as he is ready, get him to do it himself. Encourage him to look something up in an index, or to follow a route on a map.

If you travel by subway with your child, let her find the way. Show her a subway map and help her find the best route from, say, Queens to Coney Island, or wherever you happen to be going. Then get her to read the signs and work out which platform and which train you need. The same approach is good at an airport. Let kids take their time. Once they can cope with the subway, it will be far easier as an adult coming to grips with the Paris Metro, the London Subway, or any other underground system. Once kids can help find their way around a local airport, the big ones at Atlanta, Chicago, or Dallas/Fort Worth will be less daunting.

Here are some of the basic skills your children should be able to think through for themselves by the time they leave home (and in many cases well before). These are "thinking" skills here, so they are all things children will have to be able to apply to different books or train systems for themselves. You're just giving them the core skill.

- ➤ Using an index/dictionary/encyclopedia
- ➤ Using an Internet search engine
- ➤ Making a phone call to get information
- ➤ Reading a map
- ➤ Reading a timetable
- ➤ Planning a journey (including the time it will take)
- ➤ Planning a meal (picking a recipe, shopping for ingredients, following the recipe)
- ➤ Planning a trip or activity (from how to get there to what they might need)
- ➤ Organizing people to be in the same place at the same time

Lateral Thinking

It's far easier to get children to think unconventionally before they've learned to think conventionally. Our adult minds can get stuck in a rut, so now is the time to train your children to think laterally, before their brains ever discover there's an alternative.

Children can help solve the most unexpected problems. I've known elementary school–age children to explain where you're going wrong assembling Ikea furniture, work out how to get all the luggage to fit in the back of the car, and come up with a really practical way to make grandma feel special on her birthday even when you can't go and visit because it's a school day.

Teaching someone to think "outside the box" is hard once they know the box is there. If you prompt them, you are effectively taking the box away, which wasn't the point of the exercise. So the best approach is, while they're young, to get children thinking about anything and everything. Always involve them in solving problems if you possibly can, as follows:

➤ The fact that your children don't know all the constraints may well enable them to come up with an answer you couldn't see. And actually, these answers often work, or can be used as a springboard for a workable solution.

➤ Involving children in adult problems (such as where to put the sofa, or what to do about getting to school when the car has broken down) will make them feel important, and even more so if they can come up with a solution. Don't exclude them just because you think they're not interested. Even if your personal transport problem doesn't engage them hugely, they'll enjoy the chance to try a bit of problem-solving.

➤ Never pooh-pooh any idea, even if you can see it won't work. Find something in it to be positive about, and encourage your child to build on it or find other ideas.

➤ If your child is struggling to come up with something workable, helping her along is better than abandoning the exercise. So if the luggage won't fit whichever way you put it in, try throwing in a few more lateral ideas: What if we take the other car? Is there anything we can leave behind? Suppose we repack this stuff into a bag instead of a rigid case? Maybe we could all carry our coats on our laps? Perhaps we can rent fishing equipment when we get there? Let children see that they can think beyond the problem of fitting these particular suitcases into this particular trunk space.

➤ There's certainly a space for puzzle books and Sudoku for kids and so on, and if your child is interested, then do encourage him. But many children just don't enjoy this stuff and, actually, it's the way you encourage them to approach everyday problems that will really teach them to think laterally.

Decisions, Decisions

When he's two, the biggest decisions your child has to make most days are whether to have cornflakes or Cheerios for breakfast, and which pants or skirt to wear. By the time he's in his teens, he's making decisions about school subjects—decisions that might have a big impact later on. By 18, well, your child will be deluged with decisions about jobs or college, where to live, who to share an apartment with, how to spend his money, and plenty more. So you need to start training him as soon as possible.

Of course, not all two-year-olds do choose which pants or skirt to wear. Some parents make this kind of decision for them. Actually, though, you need to be getting them to make every decision they reasonably can at the earliest age possible, to prepare them for a lifetime of decisions big and small. So, please, do let your two-year-old choose her pants or skirt as well as her breakfast cereal, and let your five-year-old decide for himself what he needs to wear in the yard or garden, or whether he'll be warm enough.

Some decisions are too big for children to make, of course. You don't want to give your three-year-old the final say in which daycare she goes to, though you may want to take her to visit a few and take her reactions into account. Children feel safer when big decisions are made for them—it frees them from scary responsibility—so don't load major decisions onto small children. However, by their teens, children need to make their own decisions about school and career choices, so they need to be weaned slowly to more important decisions as childhood goes on.

As a general rule, encourage your children to make decisions for themselves. Suppose your eight-year-old has forgotten his homework until the last minute and now doesn't have time to do it before bed. Does he stay up and do it (which may mean lights out the second he gets into bed), set his alarm to get up early to do it, or leave it and apologize to the teacher the next day and offer to do it that evening? It's much better to let children make this choice themselves (with your help) than to impose a solution on them: "Right, that's it, you'll just have to get up at 6:30 tomorrow."

After all, if your child has only three more years before going to high school where there will be far more homework that needs much more complicated planning and organizing, the child needs to be getting some practice at that now, ramping up gradually. It won't be as simple as one or two short pieces of work to hand in tomorrow. There'll be several homework assignments at once—some 10-minute ones to hand in on Tuesday or Wednesday, plus a 1,000 word essay for Thursday, and an art project for the Monday after next—and more coming in almost every day. How are they going to cope with that if you've never even given them the chance to make their own decision about a late homework assignment when they were younger?

Decision-Making Techniques for Children

The most important thing you can do to help your children make their own decisions is to keep asking them questions, so they can come up with their own answers. There are lots of techniques you can teach them to use, although they won't need to use them all every time. Indeed, they will make some minor decisions pretty instinctively, but there will be bigger decisions as they get older for which they may need to use some or all of these techniques. Some of the techniques include

> **Establish the requirements**—What does this decision need to achieve? One needs to make sure everything gets taken into account. For example, the next-day's pants or skirt may need to be warm enough for a trip to the park, or old enough that you or your child won't care if they get muddy. Course offering choices when there is flex room may mean the child needs to ensure that she can still study the subjects she wants to get As or Bs in, or that in her free time she figures out how to avoid a bully no matter what. So before making a decision, one has to know what will constitute a good decision. Talk this decision-making process through with your child by asking questions.

> **Identify the options**—As with your child's forgotten homework, he could stay up late, do it in the morning, or not do it and face the music. Are there any other possibilities? Again, talk this through and ask your child if he can see an alternative. This is a good opportunity for children to practice their lateral thinking skills, too; they may think of a solution that would never have dawned on you.

59

➤ **Weigh the pros and cons**—Whether you and your child write a physical list or simply do this in your heads, it's important to see the arguments on all sides. Remember that not all arguments have equal weight. It could be that one pro might outweigh a dozen cons. For example, the detention one would get for not handing in homework might outweigh all the advantages of that course of action. So the idea is not to count them up, but to assess the overall weight of them. You'll need to help your child by asking her to come up with pros and cons, and then asking her which she thinks outbalances the other.

➤ **Worst-case scenario**—Sometimes you know perfectly well what will happen whichever course of action you take. But life isn't often that simple, and usually you're balancing risks. The child *might* get away with not handing in the homework at all—if the teacher happens to be away, or in a really good mood—but what's the worst that *could* happen? Ask your child about the likely worst outcomes so he can see whether this is a risk he wants to take.

➤ **Jettison options**—Very often you can narrow down the decision to two choices. Your child might discard the idea of doing the homework now as it's just too late and she is too tired, leaving her with a straight either/or choice: get up early, or abandon the homework and cross her fingers.

Decision making is a skill that can be learned, and you can teach it to your children very easily by giving them plenty of practice, and by asking questions so that they come up with the answers for themselves. There's only one really tricky bit: You have to let them follow through with their own decision, even if you don't agree with it.

It's not a good idea to let your teenager choose, for example, whether to come on the family vacation or not, if you're going to override him if he decides not to. (Personally, mind you, I wouldn't want to be on a family vacation with a child who didn't want to be there. It could be distinctly unpleasant.) Equally, don't give your two-year-old the run of the wardrobe if you're going to tell her at the end that she can't have the outfit she's chosen because it's not warm enough.

Of course, you can always limit your child's choices. "Here are three pairs of warm pants. Which one would you like to wear?" Just make sure you're not letting the child consider any options that you would overrule. And that includes having to let him make the decision that risks a detention or some other punishment at school. It's the only way your child will learn for next time.

Have an Opinion

My husband comes from a large family. His mother used to control them all at meal times with a long metal spoon, with which she would tap anyone on the head who misbehaved, wouldn't shut up, or who helped themselves to more than their fair share. She used to instigate discussions at the table on topical subjects—politics, ethics, or religion. Every so often she would turn to one of the children and say, "What do you think?" If the child dared to respond that he wasn't sure, she would tap him firmly on the head with her metal spoon and say, "Have an opinion!"

To be frank, I would advocate leaving the spoon out of this process. In fact, I would also excuse a small child from having an opinion on, say, foreign policy in the Middle East. However, I do think the underlying approach is a good one. Not that every mealtime should entail a compulsory debate on current affairs, but if you want your children to think for themselves, dinner-time discussions are a great way to get them started.

Obviously, when your children are small you'll instigate discussions in the simplest and gentlest way, and stick to subjects that really interest them. You can simply ask them to think about something:

> "Why do you think stores close at night time?"
> "What will happen if you put your Easter egg on the radiator?"
> "Why do children have to go to school?"

As they get older you can start asking them to think about alternatives and form a view. Pick subjects they are interested in already and see what they think:

> "Do you think dogs should live in the house or in a kennel? What makes you think that?"
> "Do you think animals should be kept in zoos?"
> "If you were in charge, how many days a week would you make school days?"

Develop Their Thinking

The family dinner table is a great place for these kinds of discussions as your children get older, along with trips in the car. But there are all sorts of other opportunities for debate. If a subject crops up that is relatively complicated, and which your child has any interest in, ask him what he thinks and why:

> "Do you reckon it was fair giving that child a detention when he was new and didn't know that particular rule?"
>
> "What makes you say that plastic bags should be banned altogether to help the environment?"
>
> "What did you think about those people taking their dog to the dog pound because they couldn't take care of it?"

Whatever he says, try gently playing devil's advocate to get the discussion going. Don't put down his point of view, but propose the alternative:

> "On the other hand, don't you think he already knew that rule from his last school?"
>
> "I can see why you would want to ban plastic bags altogether. But how would people get their groceries home if they had forgotten to bring a bag? Do you think they should be banned altogether or just charged for?"
>
> "Suppose they had kept the dog when they couldn't cope with it. Would that have been right?"

Don't hammer away at it if your child doesn't want the conversation. The fact is that children like to think, and they like to know that you're interested in their opinion. So when you pick the right topic at the right moment, they will join in, and they may come up with some creative ideas, too.

The more you do this, the more natural it will become for your children to debate a topic, develop an argument, and form and defend their own opinions. Here are a few additional pointers:

➤ Try not to direct them in any way by asking leading questions, so they're free to express their own views without fear of being put down.

➤ Encourage all their ideas, and play devil's advocate to get them defending their position more strongly.

➤ Gently let them know if they're contradicting themselves.

➤ Praise them if they come up with a particularly canny line of argument, or show a good ability to develop their ideas. "Wow! That's a tough one to argue against. Good point." Or, "That was a complicated line of thought, and you have a strong case."

➤ Let them see it's okay to change your mind in the face of a strong argument. Do this yourself from time to time, so they can see it's not embarrassing, and so they can learn the words for doing it without losing face, such as, "Okay, you have a good argument there. Maybe you're right."

The 10-Year-Old Expansion

When children reach the age of about 10, they start to become more aware of the world beyond their own life. I was born in 1961, and the earliest world event I can recall was the Apollo moon landing when I was eight. That really grabbed my attention. After that, I don't remember much for another three or four years. The majority of people will tell you, similarly, that they recall very few events if any before the age of 10. Think about your own earliest memories of events that had no impact on you that you were aware of at the time.

It's at about this age that your child may show an interest in national and world events. This is great, because it gets them thinking about all sorts of ideas, from different political stances to tricky international problems. In order to encourage this interest, let your child watch the news headlines, and encourage her to read the papers. I'm not suggesting that you should expect your 11-year-old to read *The Wall Street Journal* from cover to cover, but there are things you can do to encourage this world perspective in your children:

➤ Show your child occasional articles that you think will catch her interest, just so that holding and reading a newspaper seems like a natural thing to do. I remember showing one of my children, aged about eight, an article (complete with diagrams) about the world free-diving record, which had just been broken. Anything about new fossil or dinosaur discoveries also goes down well in my household.

➤ You may have someone you can recruit (grandparents are ideal for this) to collect newspaper clippings and send a bundle every month or so. Articles with photos go down very well with under-10s, such as a picture of the world's smallest lizard, or a volcanic eruption, or semi trucks stuck in a snow drift. Ask someone who reads a different newspaper from you if possible.

➤ If your child has a particular interest, he may well be easily persuaded to look through the relevant special interest section of the weekend newspapers. The sport or auto supplements maybe, or perhaps the home or gardening section.

➤ Children are much more likely to read news digest magazines, such as *Newsweek*, rather than a newspaper. It's smaller and everything is in easily digested short articles. Kids may start off reading just one or two sections, but it's easy for them to move on to world news.

Think It Through

Your children will be pretty well set up for life if they can think for themselves. From practical "thinking" to decision making and constructing an argument, these are vital skills. And while school and life generally will give them a bit of help as they go along, it is you who can really make the difference by encouraging them both to think for themselves and to enjoy doing so.

Let Them Lead You

It's so easy as a parent to see yourself as the leader of the family (barring the odd wrangle over which parent is boss). You're the oldest, so you take charge and the kids do what you say, all being well. And, in one sense, this setup is true. There's definitely a time and a place for the "do-as-I-say-without-question-and-now" approach.

But in a family you're the leader of a rather special team, with a very special purpose: to develop all team members to reach their maximum potential. And the way to do that will vary according to the team members' unique personalities. Whether you have one child or several, a good leader will listen to her team and adapt each task to suit the individual members.

This doesn't mean not having control or discipline or expecting respect: All the team members still have to get involved and pull their weight. It's just a case of how you go about things in order to get the best from your children, and to make the most of who they are, without trying fundamentally to change their personality and natural strengths and weaknesses.

In some ways this process is easier if you have one child. It's important to listen and not to assume that his mind ticks in the same way as yours, but if you're on the lookout for clues, they'll be easy to spot.

If you have two or more children, however, the job becomes trickier, because the automatic assumption is that you treat them all the same. In fact, however, this policy isn't necessarily the right one. There's much more in Chapter 10, "Give Them Each Other," about siblings, but this chapter concentrates on your children individually, rather than their relationship with each other.

Let Them Be Themselves

Your child will almost certainly be similar to you in many ways. After all, she is made up of 50 percent you. She may well have your natural love of music, your ability to spell, your gregarious nature, and your inclination to sulk when you don't get your own way.

Then again, she may not.

Most good and loving parents find it fairly easy to cope with their child's strengths, whether or not they share them. We often hugely admire our children for being more assertive, or better at math, than we ever were.

However, coping with other character traits we can't identify with can be quite hard, whether they're negative or simply different from ourselves. There's no real empathy, however much we wish there were. If you're prone to emotional outbursts, coping with a child who sulks can be hard—and vice versa.

Suppose your attitude to a challenge is to set your jaw and meet it head on. But your child would much rather crumble in tears. If he can't face having a filling at the dentist, or feels completely overwhelmed by tonight's homework, he'll just want to curl up in a heap and sob. It can be infuriating, not the least because you have no idea why anyone would want to react that way. Well, your child probably doesn't want to react that way either—it's just the only way he knows.

> It's crucial that we allow our children to do things their own way. If your child crumbles in the face of a tough challenge, that's okay. It doesn't make her a bad person. You can't expect her to respond otherwise just because you do.

I might add, in this example, that people who crumble at challenges do have an advantage over the rest of us, even if it doesn't seem so. They are often less driven, but that can make them more easily satisfied. As they go through life, they will be able to give up on tough challenges quite happily, while the rest of us make ourselves miserable striving for something we may never achieve. So, a trait that may appear negative can be more positive than we realize.

As parents, we often get this wrong simply through not thinking about it. If you—and maybe your partner, too—have always met challenges head on, and perhaps so have your other children, it's easy to expect it of this child, too, without realizing that you're asking too much.

And why does this matter? Because if you expect your children to do something they can't, you'll undermine their confidence—which, as you saw in the last chapter, can be very damaging in the long term. If you truly believe that your child would be happier if she learned to deal with challenges better, you can teach her in a positive way, rather than setting expectations she can't meet, at least not yet. We'll look at how to do that in a bit.

How Do Your Children See the World?

Every child has a different outlook. I have three children who have grown up in the same family, and gone to the same school. One of them is open, gregarious, and trusting. One of them is wary, and finds people quite tricky until he knows them well. One of them sees the world and its inhabitants as things to be manipulated for personal gain. (I'm working on this—it's quite scary.)

Obviously, this is a very thumbnail sketch of the way they see people and doesn't consider their outlook on the world in other ways. But it shows that every child is inherently born with a different view. I hope that all three of them (especially the last one) are growing up to treat people with respect and to care about other people's welfare. But they're all coming at it from different perspectives.

It's important to understand this point, because it means that you have to treat your children differently as a result—sometimes in almost opposite ways. For example, I need one of my children to learn to be more trusting, and another to trust less readily. Here's a good starting point:

70

➤ Do a spot check on your child's—or children's—outlook on things. How do they see other people? Their role in the family? School? Healthy living? Aim to be consciously aware of how your children see things.

➤ How do your children handle problems? How do they go about solving puzzles? How do they deal with difficult situations? Are they relentless and determined or do they crumble under pressure? Do they choose to work alone or to seek help?

➤ Think about your children's preferences. Not just whether they prefer cats to dogs, or broccoli to Brussels sprouts. But whether they prefer hanging out with one friend or several, whether they like being in their comfort zone or pushing themselves beyond it, or whether they choose friends who share their interests over ones who make them laugh.

➤ Talk to your children about their take on life. Listen to the way they talk about school or friends or pets or holidays, and get a handle on what makes them tick.

➤ Bear in mind that it won't really occur to your children until they reach, say, the second half of elementary school, that everyone else's view isn't the same as theirs.

You can, slowly and over a long time, encourage your child to see things slightly differently. But you'll struggle to change their world view significantly. A gregarious child will grow up to be a gregarious adult (if nothing goes wrong), and my manipulative child will always manipulate. I can only aim to ensure that he manipulates people for good and not ill.

71

What Is Their Motivation?

One of the effects of children creating their own world view is that they are motivated differently. You may have one child who is driven by money, while another seeks responsibility, or just approval. Again, if you have more than one child, you need to use different tools to motivate them.

If you're not wise to these differences, you'll find that one child is much more responsive than another. Tilly will always clean the car for you if you offer her a couple of dollars, while Sam refuses to do it. Maybe he's just lazy but, then again, maybe he's not really interested in earning cash. Perhaps he would have been quicker off the mark than Tilly if you had offered him an extra half hour on the computer, or if you had praised and thanked him a bit more last time he washed the car.

The way to motivate your children depends on their outlook on life, and you need to work out what it is that really makes them enthusiastic. Here are some of the most typical things that motivate children:

> **Money**—Cash rewards can work well with some children, although (as you'll see in Chapter 8, "Teach Them the Value of Money") they shouldn't be used indiscriminately.

> **Security**—A promise that things won't change can reassure some children. Suppose you want to spring-clean your child's bedroom and reorganize some of the furniture so it's more space-efficient. Some kids can be persuaded to help on the basis that if they're there with you, they can make sure you don't change anything without their consent.

➤ **Status**—It's a singularly bad idea to give one of your children senior status over another. But children who are motivated by status will want to have what their friends have, or preferably better: the trendiest fashion, the flashiest technology, or the latest bedtime. Sometimes status can be a valuable motivator for a child, even though it might not work at all on his brother or sister.

➤ **Recognition**—Some children would rather have thanks, praise, and acknowledgement than any amount of money or anything else. These children seek parental approval and will be happy simply to be noticed.

➤ **Responsibility**—This makes children feel grown-up. You can tell your child, for example, that if she can go to bed on time without being hassled all week, you'll let her go to bed half an hour later on Saturday.

➤ **Job satisfaction**—For some kids, a job well done is its own reward. So if you ask them to do something they know they're particularly good at, and let them have full control of the task, they'll enjoy doing it well. It never hurts to give them a thank you as well, of course.

➤ **Challenge**—This motivator won't work on the child who crumbles under a challenge. But if you have a child who relishes a good challenge, he may well want the chance to see whether he can be the one to figure out how to operate the new DVD player.

➤ **Freedom**—These kids generally can't wait to grow up, and appreciate rewards along the lines of being allowed to play in the yard on their own, or be in charge of their own to-do list. In terms of persuasion, rather than reward, they are more likely to complete tasks if they're allowed to do it in their own way and their own time.

It would blatantly be unfair to ask Tilly and Sam to wash the car together, and then to give Tilly $2 for it and Sam nothing but a pat on the back and a thank you. But if you're only aiming to motivate one of them, you can use a different approach. You could have offered Sam the option of extra TV time instead. Whichever you do, you need to make sure Sam, especially, knows how grateful you are to have a clean car thanks to him.

What Are Their Shortcomings, Insecurities, and Fears?

Broadly speaking, as I said earlier, your children's strengths are less likely to present a problem, whether or not other members of the family share them. It's the negative traits where you have to put in the effort. I don't necessarily mean that the traits are negative in themselves, simply that they make some aspects of life harder for your child. There's nothing wrong with being shy, say, but your child will be happier if she can overcome it, or at least control it.

The first thing you need to do is to recognize the characteristics that hold your child back in some way. You don't have to sit down now and list them all at once. Some of them won't become apparent until they're older. But you do need to make a conscious note of those traits that your child may need help keeping in check. The possibilities can be varied and numerous, but here are a few examples to give you the idea:

- ➤ Anxiety
- ➤ Lack of confidence
- ➤ Poor organization
- ➤ Stubbornness
- ➤ Shyness
- ➤ Poor concentration
- ➤ Reluctance to see things through
- ➤ Bossiness
- ➤ Negativity
- ➤ Poor ability to keep track of time
- ➤ Selfishness
- ➤ Giving up rather than taking on a challenge
- ➤ Tantrums
- ➤ Excessive fears of everyday things such as spiders, traffic, or running out of chocolate. (Hang on, sorry, that last one's mine.)

What Are You Going to Do About It?

Okay, you've established that your child is suffering because he is hopeless at organizing himself, or she's hamstrung by shyness. It's no good just sitting back and thinking, "That's a shame, poor kid. Destined to go through life with that burden."

Nope, you need to help him get over the problem. Not only because it's not okay to leave your children with such hurdles throughout life, but also because they need to see that these things can be overcome, and to start to learn for themselves how to do it. So when they become suddenly anxious after leaving home, or their poor ability to keep track of time gets to be an issue with their first job, or their lack of confidence shatters them when they have a baby, they'll have an idea of how to help themselves.

Will They Grow Out of It?

There are many character traits that will ease as your child gets older. The child probably won't lose her shyness or tendency to worry entirely, but these traits may well recede to perfectly manageable levels. So the answer may be to do nothing for now, but to watch closely and monitor, and be prepared to step in and help if necessary.

Meantime, if the topic arises, just let your child know you're not worried. Don't undermine her by saying, "You do have a problem with this," or "Gosh, how you do think you're going to cope when you leave home, if you can't even manage now?" No, obviously you weren't going to say that. I know that really. But go one step further. Tell her, "Lots of people are shy when they're children," or, "It takes time to learn to put other people first."

And, while you're at it, don't label your children. Never tell them they're shy, or an anxious person, or rubbish at managing their time. Simply acknowledge that they find it difficult to talk to new people, or cope with certain things without worrying, or get themselves organized. Doing so doesn't imply the task is beyond their capability; merely that it's a challenge for them to some degree.

Although you should show that you're not overly concerned, you shouldn't dismiss your child's feelings. He may be oblivious to the fact that he's selfish or finds it hard to concentrate. On the other hand, he may be painfully aware that he struggles more than his siblings to make new friends, for example. In that case you should acknowledge his concerns while reassuring him that he's not abnormal: "It's very scary for some people to make friends. How does it make you feel?" Let your child tell you and respond to him, and then say, "It does get easier as you get older, you know." You could also gently show him he's not alone by saying something like, "Who else in your class do you think finds it difficult, too?" Simply discussing the problem with your child shows you're not dismissing him. If it really bothers your child you should move on from waiting for him to grow out of it to actively trying to help him according to the guidelines that follow.

Who's the Best Person to Help Them?

As a general rule, it will be easiest for you—and very possibly your children, too—if they are helped by an adult who understands how they feel. If you can say, "I used to struggle with that, too, when I was your age," it will help them to open up and feel comfortable about telling you what it's like.

So, if there are two of you, see who is in the best position to help. If you're a single parent, you may have to do this yourself even if you haven't a clue as to what your child is feeling. However, there may be a grandparent, aunt or uncle, or a family friend who can help. Even if you have to do the bulk of the work yourself, it's worth tipping off a relative or friend to let your child know that she has been there—been shy, too, for instance.

Friends and family can also be a useful sounding board for you. If anyone you know has any insight into your child's problem, whether it's from when he was a child, or as a parent, teacher, or other relevant professional, why not have a quick pick at their brain? This person may come up with just the angle you need to help your child.

Just one word of warning here if your child does take after you: Empathy can only be a good thing, but don't make the mistake of assuming that what worked for you will necessarily work for your child. It might hit the spot perfectly. Then again, while list-making helped you get on top of your personal organization, it might leave her cold. So, if you have the advantage of having been in your child's shoes yourself, be especially wary of falling into this trap.

Talk to Your Child

You don't have to make a formal appointment, but neither should you assume that you can solve this issue without your child's help. If she's old enough to recognize the problem, she's old enough to play a part in solving it. So next time the subject comes up, talk to her.

What should you say? You know your own child, but the idea is to get her agreement that taking some kind of action would be helpful, and then formulate a plan of how to master the problem. Here's the gist:

➤ Start by agreeing that this issue is a challenge for her. You can say something like, "You know, all of us find some things easier than others. There are lots of things you're lucky enough to find really easy. And then there are some that take longer to learn. I wonder whether making friends/being on time/doing things you don't like/controlling your temper is one of the things that's harder work for you." Your child is not a fool, and if your analysis is correct, she'll be able to see it. She may defend her position by saying something like, "I only lose my temper because Sam keeps getting on my last nerve." But that in itself is an admission.

➤ Don't compare the child with her siblings under any circumstances. Tilly knows that Sam doesn't lose his temper when she tries to wind him up, but she doesn't want to hear it, least of all from you.

➤ Let your child know that overcoming the issue is doable: "Just because people find things more diffi-cult, it doesn't mean they can't do them. They just have to work a bit harder. It may take you a while to learn to control your temper, but you'll get there in the end." You could add, "Just like I did." If this is something you can empathize with your child over, let him know. You might even be able to add some humor (it always helps): "It was when I tipped a whole container of yogurt over your grandpa that I finally realized I had to do something about my own temper. I was eight—well, nearly nine by the time he let me out of my room."

➤ If necessary, give your child an incentive to change. If he's hopelessly unorganized, tell him about his uncle who missed out on a whole vacation once because he turned up at the airport with a passport that had expired. Tell your child that it's no fun being unable to organize oneself, so learning the basic skills is worth it.

79

➤ A good point to mention is that she is not going to be able to turn into a different person, but that she doesn't need to. She may still be shy, but she can handle it in such a way that she'll be a shy person with lots of friends. Or he can be an unorganized person who is capable of remembering to have a valid passport when he travels.

Now comes the trickiest part. You've commiserated, empathized, motivated, and encouraged—now you have to do something. Come up with some kind of technique or solution that will help. Remember that you have plenty of time, so you can try one thing for a bit, and then try something else if that doesn't work. Some children—depending on their age and the nature of the problem—will be happy to try several techniques at once. Some will want to try one thing at a time. You may need to think long and hard, pick your friends' brains, read books, and go online in order to come up with techniques. It depends on the problem and how extreme it is, and how easily ideas come to you. Crucially, you need to enlist your child's help in coming up with ideas—she will be the very best judge of what has a chance of working.

> You're not telling your child what to do here; you're just offering some suggestions to make her life a bit easier, so let her lead you as to what technique will work.

For example, if your child has a short fuse and a foul temper, you could suggest he try just walking out of the room when he's riled. When they're an adult this technique may not always work, but it's a good starting point. There'll be plenty of time, once he's mastered that, to learn how to stay in control without leaving the room. Or he might prefer to do what I used to do as a teenager (once I'd finally thought of it) when my brother teased me in order to get a rise. I faked a tantrum as soon as I could see it was only a matter of time. This kept him happy—he thought he got what he wanted—and I was still in control. You or your child might have all sorts of other ideas, too.

It might be that the solution requires some other input. Maybe you want to teach your child to meditate, or send him for judo lessons. If you and your child are both happy with this method, go for it. As always, let him take the lead. Any solution will work but only if he buys into it. Imposing your own solution will simply fail, and undermine your child's confidence at the same time.

Notice Their Achievements

Your children may resolve their problems completely, or—more likely—just take the first step toward getting them under control. Whichever they do, it's essential that you notice and give them credit: "Well done for biting your tongue—I could see you were getting hot under the collar but you held it in." Whatever you do, don't add, "Shame you couldn't have done the same thing over breakfast." Never spoil praise by adding a criticism. Besides, you shouldn't expect them to change overnight; they'll be short-tempered for years, if not forever. Your objective is not to change them but to help them. You're helping them to become a short-tempered person who can keep her lip buttoned, a shy person who can make friends, an anxious person who can get through the day happily, or a laid-back person who can see a task through to the end.

Where Will They Lead You?

One of the best things about having children is the excitement and anticipation of seeing what they'll become. It's a real privilege to have a part in helping them along the way, but it's their way and only they can choose the route and the eventual destination. If you try to take over, you'll only mess things up, however well-meaning you are. If you try to fit one child into the mold of another, or into your own format, you will fail.

The most important thing you can do for your children is to let them take the lead. Don't try to get them to be the world's most organized people, or the life and soul of the party. Don't focus on helping them get As or to become a doctor. Just focus on helping them to be happy, and everything else will follow.

Forget Quality Time

Here's a lesson I learned for myself quite unexpectedly. When my second child was born, my oldest was two. My new baby was big and hungry, and for the first few weeks I spent most of the time with him, breastfeeding him. I could read to the older one while I was doing this, but, of course, two-year-old boys prefer running around, and I couldn't very easily follow him around the house, fetch him drinks, bathe him, pick him up when he fell over, push him around on his tricycle, and play on the floor with him while I was breastfeeding. Of course, I could have done it if I'd had to—plenty of mothers manage—but I was lucky and I didn't have to because my husband had taken a month off work.

I missed spending as much time as usual with my two-year-old, so my husband and I decided that for an hour each afternoon he would mind the baby during nap time and I would have an hour of "quality time" with the older one. I'd spend an hour playing out in the garden, or doing jigsaw puzzles, or messing about with play dough. But something wasn't right. My two-year-old just wasn't comfortable, though I couldn't quite put my finger on it. There was something stilted and unnatural between us. The system just didn't work.

Then one day the baby barely slept until early evening. So by the time I got my hour off, it was time to feed the older one and put him to bed. That's what I did. It seemed a shame, because I had to be quite tough with him—he could be quite tricky about mealtimes and he hated ever getting out of the bath—and I didn't want to have to get firm when I had only a short time with him. But the extraordinary thing was that I got a completely different response from him. Suddenly he was responding normally with me, and seemed far happier and more relaxed (except about getting out of the bath, obviously).

> From that day we switched the system, and we made sure that although my time with him was limited, I used it for the routine things, not "special" activities. In other words, we stopped doing "quality time" and started doing real time instead.

Defining "Quality" Time

What my son wanted from me wasn't playtime. I mean, that's all fine, but frankly he could get that anywhere. From playgroup, from granny, from the various visitors who flocked to the house to see the new baby—and who discovered pretty quickly that the baby was much like any other and they got far more response out of the older child. And, of course, his dad, who was spending both play and routine time with him.

What he wanted from me was security. This was especially important with a new baby on the scene, but this is what children want from their parents all the time. And what gives them security? Consistency, routines, and boundaries, as you saw in Chapter 1, "Make Their World Solid." It was essential for him, as it is for all children, that I spend time with him reinforcing these things.

You can't do that on a trip to the zoo, or having an impromptu game of hide-and-seek in the garden. What's to be consistent about? Where's the routine? In order to give your children what they want, you have to do the boring routine stuff. That's what parents are for, in their eyes, and that's what counts. Getting them dressed, feeding them, putting them to bed. Those are the things that matter, and those are the times you need to be there for your kids.

Keep Boundaries in Place

It's not only the routine that is important about these activities. These are also the times when your children are most likely to step out of line. So that means you need to discipline them, and reinforce the rules. They already know the rules, of course, because these are things that crop up daily. Don't put that crayon up your nose. Don't give your breakfast to the dog. Don't pour bubble bath down the overflow. But kids need to be told these things over again. Sometimes they need to do them just to check that the rules are still there, keeping them safe.

The phrase "quality time" suggests that the most virtuous time you can spend with your children is "free time," frolicking through poppy fields or engrossed in model train sets together. This idea is hugely and damagingly misleading. Free time is great as a bonus extra, but that's all it is. The best thing you can do for your children with limited time is spend it on those boring, routine daily chores—boring in the sense that you do them day in, day out, but actually fascinating because those are the times you really get to know your kids, and the times when you build the strongest bond.

85

Your children don't need a parent for the fun, exciting stuff. But only a parent will still love them as much after a 20-minute fight to get them into the bath every single night. They need to see that you're the one who is always there for them through the tough times as well as the fun.

I know many parents who have only limited time with their kids, especially during the week. And I've noticed that the ones who spend that time doing routine things with their kids have far closer relationships with them than the ones who run around having fun with them and then leave their partner to feed the children or put them to bed.

I'm not saying that you should never play with your children, or take them to the beach. Of course you should when you can. But this is free time—not quality time—and it's a bonus, not an essential. Make the routines as fun as you can, as often as you can manage it, and you'll be a far better parent than if you get these priorities the wrong way round.

And That Goes For "Me Time," Too

There also seems to be another misguided time-related notion on the rise, and that's the idea that parents have an inalienable right to "me time." It's actually very simple: If you want to be a good parent, your child has to be more important in your life than you. This was second nature to our parents and our grandparents (at least the women); if you had offered them time off for a weekly spa treatment or an afternoon to themselves every Wednesday, they would have turned you down. Their place was with the children.

Nowadays some parents will book a vacation somewhere that has a staff able to look after the kids all day so the parents can do their own thing. This seems terribly sad; young children are desperate for their parents' company on vacation, and the best parents want to spend their time with the kids, because that's much more fun than anything else they could be doing.

I'm not saying you should never have any time alone, or with your partner. If you leave the kids in the daycare center for one morning on your week's vacation, and they are okay with that, then it's fine. But me time (the term itself indicates what a self-ish concept it is) is a lucky bonus you get on a good day after the kids are in bed, or once they go to school (if you don't work full time), or during a weekend if you have a partner to give you a couple of hours' break.

When you decide to have children, you give up your right to me time. It's no good telling the kids that they can't do ballet because it clashes with your yoga session, or that you and your partner are leaving them with friends or relatives for a few days because you're off on a romantic trip.

Of course you can get a babysitter and go out for an evening, and of course you can say, "I'll do that for you in a minute; I'm just having a quick cup of coffee and a break first." You shouldn't be a slave for the kids. But the bottom line is that whether you're having to compromise your hobby, your career, your vacation, or your free time, the children's needs are more important than yours.

After all, thinking it through, if you don't do this, you're sending the children a clear signal that the way to live your life is to put yourself before everyone else, including your nearest and dearest. That won't actually make them happy, and those aren't the sort of values you want to impart (as you saw in Chapter 3, "Show Them How to Separate Right from Wrong").

Making the Most of Your Time

All right, so we've abandoned the notion of quality time and me time. That free time is great when you have it, but it's not the really important time to spend with them. But how much time should you spend playing with them, and what should you be doing with it?

This is where having more than one child is a big advantage. Sure, you have to put up with all the squabbles and the fighting, but broadly speaking your children will entertain each other, barring the interruptions to referee fights.

If you have only one child (or more than one, but so far apart in age that they aren't playmates), every time she wants a companion, it's you. If she wants to play any card game other than solitaire, you have to play it with her. If he wants someone to pretend to be a tiger, or to help build a den, it's up to you.

Actually, however, it's far better for your child to play with other children. Of course, he needs some time with you, but all children should get enough of that in normal family life—bedtimes, mealtimes, holidays, and so on. Playing is something best done with other kids.

However hard you try, above the age of about 18 months you just can't give a child as much of what she needs as another child can. Even if you can resist the temptation to lead her game in the way you want it to go (which few adults really can), you just aren't giving the child a chance to learn about social interaction. Children need to learn to share, to resolve differences, to listen to each other's ideas, to resist being bossy, and all those other people skills. You can't help them there. Either you'll capitulate because, frankly, you don't care who has the blue playing piece and who has the green one, or you'll pull rank on them and tell them how it's going to be. Even if you try to share decisions with them, you'll be reasonable and rational in a way that other children wouldn't.

What smart parents of single children do is to get them spending as much time with other children as possible. They enroll them in playgroups and nurseries, invite school friends over to play, and let neighbor children come around as much as they can.

If you have more than one child, then it's a good idea to keep out of their way as much as possible. They'll let you know when they need you, but actually you'll never make as convincing a monster as a brother, and you always have to have the rules explained to you because you don't know the back story. So your child would much rather play with his sibling given the choice. Not all the time, but most of it. And that's a good thing. So don't feel guilty about doing the laundry or fixing that broken window while they play.

Get the Focus Right

Sometimes, however, they (and you) will want to spend time doing something with each other. That's where real life gets so irritating. Your children want you to join in a game, need you to show them something, or to help them. However, you still have a hundred and one chores to get done before they go to bed. Those are the times when we only half listen to them: "Hmmm? Oh, that's nice, darling...." Or when we get cranky, "Yes, I know you need help, but look at all this laundry. And the kitchen table is a mess, thanks to you...."

Recognize that scenario? Of course you do. Up to a point, your child has to understand that there are days when the amount of work has already expanded beyond the time available by 10 o'clock in the morning. Sometimes you just don't have time for more than a cursory helping hand.

But what about all those mornings, afternoons, or evenings when you find yourself slightly stressed and unable quite to concentrate on the kids or the chores? They want you to give them their full attention, and clearly intend to keep asking until they get it, while you would like to oblige but if you don't get the dinner on it won't be cooked before bedtime.

The answer here is to focus fully on one thing, and then the other. In fact, to be specific, you need to focus on the chores first, and explain to your children:

> "If you leave me alone until I get the meal in the oven, I'll be able to give you a clear 20 minutes before I have to clean the kitchen. But if you keep hassling me it will take me longer and I won't have 20 minutes for you at the end of it."

You need to do it this way, because if you give them their 20 minutes first, there's no guarantee they'll leave you alone after that. This way, everyone benefits, and you'll feel much less stressed. You may be brilliant at multitasking, but that doesn't mean you necessarily enjoy it. So do one thing first and then the other.

Your children want your attention (unless they're otherwise distracted, in which case you're dropped instantly). That doesn't change from when they're tiny until when they leave home. But they would rather have your full attention if they can get it (though partial attention is better than nothing), so in my experience they will pretty well always agree to this. The other proviso, of course, is that you stick to the bargain; otherwise, they won't believe you next time. So, if they hassle you, don't give them their time even if you find you are 20 minutes ahead of yourself. And if they leave you alone, give them 20 minutes somehow even if you're behind schedule.

Share Your Attention

Well, that all sounded pretty easy. But hang on, what's happening now? Sam wants you to help get the bikes out from under a pile of boxes in the garage, but Tilly needs help with her homework. And you only have time for one of them. What are you going to do?

Look, I don't know the answer. All I can tell you is that in the long run it's good for your children to learn to share your attention, as long as you divvy it up fairly. After all, they have to share their friends' attention, and if they have children themselves, they'll have to share their partner's attention. So it's not a bad thing that it happens now and they can get used to it. The question is, how do you handle it?

91

Each situation is slightly different, but some general guidelines should help to make sure none of your children grows up thinking that he got less of you than his siblings:

> ➤ The important thing is to be seen to be fair (whether or not you're actually giving them equal time).

> ➤ Some requests for input are a call for attention, while others are genuinely practical. Maybe Tilly can help Sam with the bikes while you're busy, and then you'll use your few precious spare minutes to help Tilly with her homework. Or did Sam actually want *you*, rather than help with the bikes? If you stop and think about this, you can usually work out the answer. Certainly if your child is asking for help with something he can do perfectly well without you, it's probably attention he wants. If it's something he can't do alone, it may well be straightforward help he needs (and therefore not necessarily from you).

> ➤ Maybe both kids just need assistance, but there still isn't time for them both. In that case, consider whose need is most urgent. If the homework has to be done and Sam doesn't *have* to take the bike out, I think you had better help Tilly this time.

> ➤ Make sure they understand why you've picked the child you have. The crucial thing they need to know is that it isn't because you love Tilly more than Sam. It's only because Tilly's homework has to be in tomorrow. Remind Sam how long you spent slaving over his history homework last weekend.

> ➤ Apart from urgent problems, try to share yourself round as fairly as you possibly can.

> ➤ Remember that some children need more attention than others. So if you're assessing fairness on the basis of need, the way to be fair may not be to give them equal time.

If you have two children and a partner who is around a lot, attention-divvying problems may not arise that often because your partner and you can often attend to one child each. Try to make sure it isn't always Dad who helps the big one and Mom the little one, or something of the sort.

However if you have more than two children, or are a single parent with more than one, this problem is going to happen a lot. Likewise it will happen if your partner is at work or away a lot of the time, leaving you alone with the kids. But remember that your children will think this is normal, and don't expect to have your undivided attention for long periods very often (except maybe at bedtime). They've probably shared you ever since they can remember.

Don't Believe the Soft-Focus Fantasy

There's a popular myth that is guaranteed to arouse feelings of guilt in almost any parent, and that's "The Waltons"-style, advertisement sort of image of parents spending hours giggling and playing happily with their kids. Baking cakes and dabbing little puffs of white flour on the ends of their cute little noses, and skipping around the kitchen while waiting for the baking to cook, before icing the delicious cupcakes beautifully in pink and white icing.

This fantasy is okay, it's not just you. It doesn't actually happen like this for anyone else either. It's a myth. Just occasionally it goes like this, but only maybe once or twice a year at best—and that's for parents with the free time to do it. If you're a single parent with a full-time job, I reckon you're doing well if you can achieve this fantasy once in your kids' entire childhood. I mean, yes, obviously you'll attain this nirvana for the occasional five-minute burst, until the squabbling breaks out over who licks the spoon. But you can't make it last for the entire time it takes to make, bake, and frost a batch of cupcakes.

If this scenario is going to work at all, there are certain conditions you must be able to fulfill. If you can't, don't raise your expectations to dreamy, rose-tinted levels. Expect stress and squabbles, and just hope you can keep them to a minimum. Here are the conditions you need in order to stand any chance of an afternoon in parenting dreamworld:

➤ You must have far more time than you think you could possibly need.

➤ You must not care if the cupcakes turn out inedible and look revolting.

➤ You must not care, in fact, if the cupcakes never get made at all.

➤ You must be perfectly happy to do whatever cleaning up is needed, probably on your own.

➤ For a lot of activities, including cooking, you must have only one child with you.

This is not a set of conditions it is possible to meet very often, which is why most of these activities end in disappointment. A dear friend was telling me recently about a frustrating afternoon spent with her twins trying to clean a hand-me-down collection of Legos with warm soapy water. She explained that her problem was that she wanted the Legos to end up clean, which wasn't what her toddlers wanted at all. With hindsight, she reckoned, she should have given them half a dozen pieces to "wash," while she quietly cleaned all the rest of it herself.

There she had hit on the crux of the thing: She and her children had entirely different requirements. What she wanted out of the exercise wasn't what they wanted out of it. And that's the key to it. Being a first-class parent, she did the decent thing and played it their way—and washed the Legos properly later.

You see, actually, as long as your children are getting what they need out of the activity, you're doing the best you can for them. You may not be achieving that (unattainable) fantasy of perfect parenthood, but you're giving the children your attention, which was what they actually wanted, and you're letting them direct the activity.

Your children's primary need here is for your attention, and preferably the non-stressed version, which is why it works so much better if you start off assuming the cookies or cupcakes will be inedible, or the Legos will end up dirtier than when you started. Once you've grasped that, you'll still get frustrated at the amount of water or flour that's ending up on the floor, and—yikes—you're going to have to change your slacks now, and they'll probably degenerate into squabbling eventually, but just enjoy the moment, and don't expect it to last right through until the cupcakes are iced.

Oh, and if you actually want to bake some cupcakes, do it when the kids aren't around.

Balance Time and Attention

The time you spend with your children and the attention you give them aren't exactly the same thing, but they're interlinked. It's sometimes a tricky balance dividing your time between the kids and all the other things you have to do. None of us gets it right all the time.

Just aim to give your children real time before "quality" time, and to give them your full attention when you can, even if that means a period of no attention (barring emergencies) while you get everything else done. And make sure that when you do have time for activities together, you think about what the children want out of it, rather than trying to achieve something that won't happen and they don't care about anyway.

Make Sure You See the Forest *and* the Trees

It can be infuriating when your six-year-old still won't use a knife and fork to eat. Or your 12-year-old can't pack his school bag on his own without forgetting half the things he needs. Sometimes you want to scream at your kids for the mess they leave lying around, or their inability to think ahead, or to hold a conversation with an adult without clamming up.

The key thing to keep in mind, for your sake as well as theirs, is that you have 18 years to prepare them for the big wide world. When you despair of them, step back and look at how far you've come (at least you're not spoon-feeding your six-year-old any more) and how far you still have to go (she does need to learn to use the knife properly).

It's important that you pace yourselves here—both you and your child. It's not fair or necessary to pile on the pressure so that your children are fully independent by the age of seven, but neither is it fair to send them out into the world unable to use a washing machine or to eat a meal in public without disgracing themselves. So the best thing you can do for your children is to concentrate on the immediate objective without losing sight of the final target.

One Small Step Versus One Giant Leap

Your children should be able to do all sorts of things happily and independently by the time they leave home. We look at some of them in a bit. Almost every one of these skills is made up of many small steps. For example, let's consider the laundry. It really isn't fair to your children not to equip them with the ability to keep their own clothes clean once you're not there to do it for them. But it's not a matter of waiting until they're 16 and then suddenly panicking and making them learn the whole thing from scratch (at the same time as learning all the other things you're panicking about, plus coping with the hormones, the homework, and everything else).

You need to take the teaching of this task in stages. As kids get older, they need to learn to do the following in an order that suits you, but here's an example:

1. Put their dirty clothes in the hamper.

2. Put their clean, folded clothes back in their closet or dresser.

3. Take the dirty laundry to the washing machine.

4. Load the washing machine, put in the washing detergent, and turn on the machine to a basic wash.

5. Take the laundry out of the machine and hang it up, or put it in the tumble dryer.

6. Fold up the dry laundry.

7. Use an iron safely and without making the clothes more creased than when they started (I think I still need to work on this one personally—not enough practice, I suspect).

8. Separate out clothes that need special treatment—cool wash, no spin, hand wash, dry clean.

9. Use different settings on the washing machine.

10. Hand wash clothes.

I hope you won't get picky with me if your child can do things in a different order, or you don't use a tumble dryer, or whatever—I'm sure you get the gist here.

The point is that if you start getting your toddler to put clothes in the laundry basket, and then encourage him at preschool age to carry the clothes to the washing machine, and by school age to put his own clothes back in the closet or dresser, he's already well on his way toward learning a new skill.

Take Stock

Where some of us fall short is that we pat ourselves on the back, quite rightly, for getting to a certain point with teaching the kids a useful skill, and then nothing more happens for years. Suddenly you realize when the kids are in their mid-teens that they still don't know how to wash clothes (sometimes even an item or two by hand) or take their red T-shirt out before the wash goes in the machine. And if you never told them, it's really not their fault.

So it's important to keep monitoring all those essential skills and make sure that you're about the right distance down the road to your target of having them self-sufficient at 18. You don't need to keep a detailed list of every skill, broken down into its component parts, and tick them all off as you go. I guess that would work, but it's too military and humorless for my taste. It's just a matter of noting from time to time what the essential skills are, and mentally reflecting on

> ➤ How far they've come
> ➤ How far they still have to go
> ➤ Whether they're lagging behind and you both need to put some extra effort in
> ➤ What the next stage in the process will be

Don't Wait Too Long

Bear in mind that the later in their lives you leave teaching these things, the harder it can be for your children to learn them. That doesn't mean you should have taught them all they need to know before they start school, but you want to keep pretty much on track. If you've allowed your teenager to drop his dirty clothes on the floor for you to pick up ever since he could undress himself, it will be pretty tricky, teenagers being what they are, suddenly to persuade him to deal with the laundry himself. If, on the other hand, he's already putting a load of laundry through himself from time to time, then encouraging him to wash a few items by hand won't be nearly so hard.

Teaching Techniques

So how are you going to teach your children these things? Teaching them to put their dirty clothes in the hamper is not hard. *Getting* them to do it might take a while, but it's not as if they don't know how. But what about teaching them to clean out the rabbit cage, or to organize their homework due dates? These kinds of tasks can be pretty daunting to a child who has never done it before. It's no good just telling them to get on and do it.

There's a four-stage process to teaching your child (or anyone else) this kind of skill:

1. You do it while she watches.
2. You both do it together.
3. She does it while you watch or check.
4. She does it alone.

If you're teaching a 10-year-old to clean out the rabbit cage, this technique will do the trick pretty swiftly. But don't assume that you have to do each of these stages only once. Suppose your child is naturally pretty unorganized, and has to pack his backpack for school each day with all the right books. Plus, when he has art he needs to remember, say, an apron. Oh, and his recorder for music. And his reading book on the days he has English.

When your child is in late elementary or middle school, you might pack his bag for him every day for a while until he gets settled in. Then for a while you might do it together. And once he starts doing it for himself, you may need to check it for him afterward for another short while. And remind him to do it for a while after that.

> Just keep your eye fixed on the forest, not the trees: The aim is to get him self-sufficient once he leaves home. You still have several years left—it's okay to take a year or more to perfect this skill.

Everyone's Different

Your next child might insist on packing her own bag by herself from day one. And she might get it right every time. You can't expect both or all your children to learn things at the same speed. It's irrelevant what any other child is doing, and comparison shouldn't enter the equation.

So don't compare your children, especially not to their faces: "Why can't you get it right? Your sister could do this when she was two years younger than you are." I'm sure you're not going to say anything quite that ill-advised. After all, so what? I bet there are some things at which this child is way ahead of her prissy sister. If you compare your children you'll not only cause unhelpful sibling resentment, you'll also undermine and pressurize the slower child, and frustrate yourself by raising your expectations too high.

Deal with each child individually. One of them may moan to you, "It's not fair, I have to keep my room clean but Sam's room is always a mess and you don't make a fuss. And Sam's older than me." Well, this situation is tricky, but it's not impossible. Just explain that everyone finds some things easier to learn than others, and you expect your children to do what they're capable of. Praise this child for her ability to be tidy, and point out that Sam is expected to try just as hard, but is taking longer to perfect it. Then draw her attention to something she finds harder than Sam does. Don't mention the comparison with Sam—she'll work that out for herself—just say, "You find being tidy fairly easy, but I give you quite a lot of leeway about helping with the shopping because I know that's a bigger challenge for you."

Be Their Memory Jogger

It's worth recognizing that when it comes to children doing jobs such as putting away their toys or feeding the goldfish, there are three stages to go through:

1. You do it for them.
2. You remind them to do it.
3. They do it without being reminded.

Expecting children to remember to do things for themselves as soon as they have mastered the skill isn't reasonable. If you expect that, you'll get constantly frustrated and find yourself nagging them. Research has shown that people who are nagged are actually *less* likely to do the thing than if they aren't nagged. Besides, no one wants to be a nag anyway.

However, if you expect to remind them, and see doing so as part of your role, you won't mind doing it and you'll be much less stressed about it. And when you remind them, you'll do it in a friendly tone rather than exasperated one. You may need to remind them for just the first few weeks, or you may need to remind them for a couple of years, depending on their age and personality, and the task in question.

When you think it's time your children did a task without being reminded, talk to them about it. You'll probably know when the time comes because when you remind them they usually say, "Done it!" But they still need to know that you'll be expecting them to do it without a reminder in future.

Cleaning Their Rooms

I want to make a special mention of cleaning for two reasons. One is that it is a skill that most parents expect their children to have innately and they don't, but it can be taught. I'll come back to that in a minute.

The other reason is that this task is probably the biggest area of conflict when it comes to teaching your child skills for life. Few children choose to keep their bedroom perfectly clean at all times without being asked—even, or perhaps especially, older children and teenagers. Some parents expect their children to keep their bedrooms immaculate. Others believe it's the child's bedroom and they're entitled to keep it in whatever state they like—and anyway, it's not worth the battle to get them to clean it. Most of us fall somewhere between the two, and expect a certain level of cleanliness, or want the room picked up every so often so it can be properly cleaned.

Which of these camps you fall into is your business. But if you want to prepare your child for adulthood, this skill is one they need to have. That doesn't mean, however, that it is necessarily a skill they have to *use*. It isn't fair to let your children leave home incapable of keeping their room/desk/workspace/house/garage clean. This lack will handicap them when they come to get a job working alongside other people, or share an apartment with a friend.

Once you've taught them the skill, however, it's up to you whether you demand that they use it routinely. You owe it to your children to make sure that they *can* have a clean room. But it's between you and them whether you insist that they *do* have a clean room.

This principle applies to many other skills, from being organized to doing the laundry. The crucial thing is that they *can* do it. It's a matter of personal choice whether you insist that they do it every time.

How to Clean

Many adults struggle to stay clean, and many of those who are naturally tidy-minded are unaware of the skills they are using. If you're going to teach your children to keep their rooms clean, you need to know what skills to give them. One of the reasons many children don't clean their rooms is because they don't know how to. One look at the task and they feel so daunted and have no idea where to start that they just want to burst into tears. (I've done it myself.) So here's a rundown of the basics:

> ➤ **Everything must have a place**—Half the problem is that your child picks something up, has no idea what to do with it, and therefore puts it down again. She

may waste time picking the object up several times, and she won't clear the mess because they have nowhere to clear it to. So make sure kids have a place—a table, box, or space on the floor—to put everything that they don't know where it goes. Once everything else has been tidied they come back to this, last of all, and deal with it. It may prompt them to decide "I need a place to keep broken things I haven't got around to fixing," or "I need somewhere to put spare rubber bands." Once you know what you need, it's easy then to allocate some space for it.

➤ **Have a trash can or trash bag, if the situation has gotten bad**—This can help children to clear out junk, because it's a lot quicker just to trash it than to fit it into a full cupboard or work out what else to do with it. And it's a big motivator when things have reached crisis point on the mess front to see how many trash bags they can fill. This is also a useful time to say, "Is there anything here somebody else might want?" and then help them put true junk into different bags from items that might go to Goodwill or to a recycle center. It's a great opportunity to enlighten your children to the idea that just because they don't want something any more, somebody else might.

➤ **Group related objects**—This step should be the first main thrust. Ideally your child should start with the biggest category here, in order to achieve the most effect fastest, which is great for morale. So, if the floor is littered with Lego pieces (as it always is in my oldest son's room), have the child put those into the relevant cupboard/drawer/plastic box first. If there are clothes everywhere, have her hang those up. If there are books all over the place, have her put them back on the shelf. Then she can move on to the next stage once the main objects are cleared.

➤ **Clear specific areas of the room**—Things should be looking encouragingly clearer now, and the light at the end of the tunnel should be visible. Now your child needs to concentrate on clearing specific places: the bedside table, the desk, the floor. Do these areas one at a time, tidying all the objects there—bearing in mind they shouldn't look too bad by now as the Legos, clothes, books, or whatever have already gone.

➤ **If the mess is significant, tackle it in stages**—Once you reach this point, you can take breaks if you want to. Aim to clear the floor now and leave the desk until after lunch. Or do the half of the room nearest the window today and the rest tomorrow.

Once you have taught your children how to clean a room—by showing them first, then doing it with them, then being alongside while they do it themselves—they should find the task far less daunting in the future. Again, if you start teaching them when they're five, they may be 15 before they finally have it cracked without any help. That's fine.

The final thing to teach your children is that little and often makes life far easier. If they put everything away as they go, they won't ever be faced with such a daunting task again. I should add that your children already know this. They may be messy but they aren't stupid. However, they will need your help to get into the habit. Remind them at bedtime each night to hang up their clothes and put their toys away. You can maybe even do the odd thing for them while they clear away something else, just until they get in the swing of it.

You Can't Fight Nature

Some children will always be messy, and I know plenty of adults who can't keep their rooms clean as they go along, so take your children's personalities into account and don't expect miracles. And again, pace yourself. You—and they—have until they're 18 to master this skill, so don't pile on the pressure unnecessarily.

Remember that you can't change their personalities. You won't make a messy child into a tidy one. She'll only ever be a messy person who has hung up her clothes—in much the same vein as an alcoholic who hasn't had a drink for 20 years. Equally, your unorganized child will only ever become an unorganized adult who has remembered to bring her passport on vacation with her.

Your job is to make sure your kids have the skill of organizing. Once they turn 18, it's their choice whether they use this skill. But at least you'll know that you haven't let them down, and if they need that particular ability they can call on it.

What Are You Trying to Achieve?

There are tons of skills, I'm afraid, that your children need to have under their belt once they leave home. However, they will learn a lot of them with very little effort on your part. If you're consciously on the alert, you should be fine on picking up on what skills they lack. It's a matter of registering when something needs doing and making sure you're not missing teaching them anything.

Sometimes you may look at your child and think, "What have I been doing? She's eight and she doesn't know how to answer a phone! How did I let this happen?" That will alert you to do something about it, and to think about any related skills you might want to teach her now or before too long—how to make a call, how to look up a number in the phone book, how to play messages back. If you want to spot these things, and are on the lookout, you will spot them. And it may well make you think that, actually, this would be a good moment to teach her younger brother, too.

Maybe a friend mentions that when she left home she didn't know how to boil an egg. That should prompt you to run a mental check of which of your children can boil an egg—or make a basic pasta dish, or cook a roast. Think about how far your children are down that particular road, and whether you need to teach them the next skill or two.

Perhaps you notice another child doing something very different from yours. For example, you discover that he's already walking to the store on his own. This will make you question whether your child should learn to do the same, or at least make more progress toward it.

On the other hand, maybe someone else's child is way behind yours. She still expects the crusts cut off her sandwiches at the age of seven while yours always eats the crusts, or at least just leaves them on the plate. Well that's one up to speed, and you can feel (privately) smug. But if you're really focused on getting your child up to speed, it will also help you remember to assess the rest of your child's eating skills. Can he sit properly at the table? Can she use a knife? Do your kids at least take their empty plate as far as the sink, even if they don't wash it up yet?

> You see, if you're consciously aware of the need to keep all these different skills progressing over the years, you won't miss much. Just keep a lookout for areas that might need work, and you'll be fine.

If you want to conduct a basic assessment now, here is a list of skills to think about. Remember that almost all of them can be broken down into lots of component parts. If your children are fairly young, you still have plenty of time and may only need to move another step or two at the moment. If you have a 17-year-old, feel free to panic if you aren't pretty close to ticking most of these off. No list can possibly be conclusive, but these are some of the essential skills kids will eventually need to be able to carry out with no help from you. In no particular order:

- ➤ Having some sense of order in their life and their possessions
- ➤ Being tidy
- ➤ Assembling what they need for school or other activities
- ➤ Getting up in the morning (that is, without your having to prod them)
- ➤ Organizing their time
- ➤ Doing their homework
- ➤ Eating like a grown-up
- ➤ Basic cooking
- ➤ Clearing and washing up after a meal
- ➤ Keeping themselves clean and maintained
- ➤ Keeping their clothes clean
- ➤ Keeping their room/apartment/house clean
- ➤ Looking after their possessions
- ➤ Looking after their own pets if they have any
- ➤ Packing for a vacation
- ➤ Household skills such as changing a light bulb, mending a fuse, reading instructions (coping with spiders?)
- ➤ Maintenance skills like sewing on a button, mending a tear, mending anything broken
- ➤ Being road safe
- ➤ Using public transportation
- ➤ Doing basic shopping
- ➤ Looking after their own money
- ➤ Basic budgeting
- ➤ Using a lawnmower, vacuum cleaner, dishwasher, washing machine

➤ Basic housework—cleaning a room, cleaning windows, and so on
➤ Cleaning and looking after a car
➤ Planning food shopping and requirements
➤ Remembering birthdays of key people and buying gifts

Emotional Preparation

There's one more huge category of skills, which can be the trickiest to teach. Your child needs lots of emotional skills to enjoy life. Some of them are covered elsewhere in this book. None of them is as simple as saying to your child, "Then you push this red button here, and the machine starts to fill with water." Oh no, that would be too easy.

All children need building up emotionally in order to get the best out of life. They all need confidence, self-esteem, assertiveness, and so on. Most children need very little help in some areas, and plenty in others. These are all skills that you need to help them develop over the whole 18 years you have them for, and it will be a slow drip in many cases.

> If you push too hard, you'll make things worse.
> If you don't push at all, they won't learn.

Suppose your child is very shy. If you never make her face tricky social situations, she'll grow up to be a very shy adult. If you force her to go to every party she's invited to, she'll just panic and withdraw and the whole social thing might become an insurmountable problem for her. So you need to go ever so slowly. Encourage her to go only to small parties with good friends when she's four or five, and stay with them. As she gets a bit older, judge the stage at which you can leave, or you can persuade her to go to bigger parties. Gradually get her used to talking to adults as well. Keep telling yourself you have 10 years left (or whatever) and there's no need to rush it.

One of the particularly tricky things about teaching this set of skills is that, unlike traveling by bus or using a vacuum cleaner, you may never have learned them yourself. You may have been born brave, or positive-minded, or gregarious, and all you ever needed was half-decent parents who didn't undermine your natural inclinations. You may not know what it's like to be shy, or bossy, or short-tempered. Of course, that means you make an excellent role model, but it doesn't help you empathize with your child.

If this is the case, talk to other people who have a better understanding. Maybe your partner, or one of your parents or friends. Find out what helped them, and what hindered them.

And talk to your children, too. Well before they're 10, say, they'll have noticed whether they find certain things much harder than their friends do. Obviously, don't tell them, "We both know you're horrible at this," but you can say, "Do you sometimes find it hard to stay patient when your friends are irritating you?" Then you can talk to them about strategies for biting their tongue, or at least expressing themselves more amenably.

Make sure you chat to other parents and observe their children. Your child may not be as far behind as you think. Just about all two-year-olds are lousy at sharing, or at chatting confidently with strangers. A lot of these things are just a natural part of growing up. What you need to keep an eye out for are those traits that are much more marked than their peers and that your kids probably need help with to get back on track.

Woodland Management

So the most important thing you can do for your children is to control the speed at which they learn vital skills. Never forget the ultimate aim for each skill, and keep the speed as steady as you can. Don't rush them before they're ready, and don't leave things so late they have more to learn than they can cope with in the last few years.

Bear in mind that being a teenager is very tough—you probably remember it yourself. There's lots of pressure at school, especially if you're aiming to get good grades. There are lots of important decisions to make about what to do with the next part of your life. You're full of hormones and find it harder to communicate. You want to be independent but you're scared of it, too. You're generally pretty confused, in fact. And anyway, it's just not cool to do what your parents tell you.

This means that the teenage years are not a good time suddenly to expect your children to start taking over loads of household chores when they've been coddled for the last 12 years.

115

So make sure that you're simply adding to existing skills, not starting from scratch. A 10- or 12-year-old should be quite capable of putting a load of laundry through the machine or doing his own packing (if you check it), so why not get him doing it now instead of springing it on him when he's 15? Learning how to do a task is so much easier if it's broken down into steps and if your parents have talked you through what to do and why from an early age.

All parents miss the odd skill here and there, but you can easily pick up on what skills your children are lacking in if you're on the lookout. The important thing is to make sure you stand back and monitor where your children are at, in relation to where they came from and where they're heading. In other words, make sure you can see both the forest *and* the trees.

Teach Them the Value of Money

When your children finally grow up and leave home, you don't want them getting into debt. Very possibly you want them not only staying out of debt but also not wasting their money, or spending when they could be saving. Nor do you want them to be insensitive toward other people who have less than they do, whether it's a friend on a lower salary, or a child starving on the other side of the globe.

Give Them Some Money So They Can Start to Understand It

It's not as if the kids aren't costing you enough already. But, yes, it is the norm to give your children money as well. You could insist they have only what they can earn (which is pretty tough when they're small), but the vast majority of parents do give their children an allowance or money in some form. We look at earning money later on.

117

Certainly your children need to have some money sooner or later if they're going to learn the value of it. So, unless you're going to make them earn every penny, how are you going to give it to them?

There are several ways to move your hard-earned money out of your own wallet and into your freeloading kids' pockets. All of them have some merits, and suit different kids and different ages. There's a strong case for progressing through these different ways as your kids develop, with some running in parallel at times. Here's a roundup of the options you're most likely to be using or considering, and when they're most appropriate.

Give Pocket Money

Giving your children pocket money is the simplest and most straightforward approach. You give them a fixed amount, an allowance, each week, or maybe each month, and they spend it as they wish. If you have more than one child you may give them the same amount, or vary it according to age. Some parents give a modest amount and then buy their children the occasional extra treat, such as a toy when they're on vacation, while others give more and expect their children to buy their own extras.

When children are young, this can be a very good system. It's simple and they understand it. It's very good for teaching small children that 20 cents won't buy a Mars bar (not any more), and it's something for them to hand over in the stores and get change from. However, as they get older you find that it's not teaching them a lot. Money manifests from nowhere, in effect,

118

and keeps being replenished when they have spent it. There's not much chance to budget because, unless your pocket money is considerable, the kids are only buying candy, comics, and the odd toy. The money doesn't last long, but then it gets replaced pretty swiftly anyway.

Let Them Earn Interest

One of the things we want to encourage our children to do is to save rather than spend. The way to do so is twofold: They need to see the benefit, and they need to form the habit. The interest system achieves both of these objectives.

Rather than paying pocket money, I offer to look after the money of my elementary school/pre-teenage children and pay them interest instead of pocket money. I pay them at a rate that they would never get from a real bank (and I make sure they know this), but then I'm using the system to generate income for them as I'm not giving them anything else. Also, I want them really to feel the benefit in order to see that saving is a lot more lucrative than spending. Most children can grasp this system from the age of about eight, but if you introduce it to all your children simultaneously, as I did, a child a couple of years younger than that may well get a sufficient grasp of it. If the younger one is confused, ask the older siblings to explain it (once they understand it themselves)—they'll probably do a better job of it than you.

Here's how it works. I'm no accountant so I keep the math pretty simple. They give me all the money they want to "bank." We started just after Christmas in my family so they all had a bit of money they had been given by relatives. I then do exactly what a bank does—I go off and spend the money myself. All the calculations are done on paper—just as with a bank—and if they want to cash in on any of it I have to provide the hard cash/ credit card to do so.

At the end of each month, I add up everything in their "account" (having kept a tally during the month of any money in or out). I then calculate interest at 10% on the first $100, and 5% on everything above that, and add it on. So if they end the month with $100, I add on $10. If they end it with $200, I add on $15. Because I give them no pocket money, this seems a reasonable amount, especially because they're saving it. After all, if they spend it all, they lose out. Suppose one of them buys something big and drops back down to $30. In that case this child will get only $3 that month, which isn't much these days. In fact, they all save really well, and always choose to reinvest their interest. About once a year they'll buy something big they've wanted for a long time, usually making sure they still have plenty left in the "bank" to earn interest.

This system really encourages saving, and makes them think twice before they splurge on something they don't really need. Because all the calculations are done on paper, they have grasped the principle that money can change hands without any cash being involved. My only real worry is that there'll be a run on the bank just when I'm having a thin month personally.

This system is a good one to progress to after straight allowance pocket money. You can, of course, run both in parallel rather than stop the pocket money. You might reduce it, or pay a lower rate of interest than I do. They could just save money they're given for birthdays from aunts and uncles, at a lower rate, or they could choose to invest their pocket money in the "bank."

Pay an Allowance

As your children get older, even interest earning will have its limitations, because it won't teach them to budget for themselves. The best way to do that is to give them an allowance and make them learn to use it wisely. Generally speaking, this is appropriate for teenage children and is most often used to pay for things which, up until now, you have been paying for. Well, you still are, of course, but they're making the decisions now.

Clothing is one of the most common forms of allowance. You assess how much you spend on clothing your children, and give them the money to spend on clothes as they wish. This is a great way to teach your children to look after their own money, and can be used as they get older for all sorts of other things than clothes—music, cell phone, going out, movies—in fact most things that they want and you're paying for at present.

There are a few things you need to take into account here (or should I say "make allowances" for?):

➤ You and your child need to be absolutely clear what the allowance covers. Are they supposed to pay for their own school uniform, sports gear, ballet outfit, and so on, or just leisure clothes?

➤ If you want to make any restrictions, agree on them clearly in advance with your child; for example, the clothing allowance can't be spent on low-cut tops, or the going out allowance can't be used for alcohol. Think these through carefully before you set up the system, or you'll rightly have an argument on your hands if you try to impose new conditions later.

➤ Agree as to what happens if there's allowance left over. Is your daughter allowed to spend less on clothes in order to go overboard with a cell phone

121

bill? Generally speaking, this ought to be fine as she's learning to prioritize her own money, but you might want to agree on specific items of clothing she must buy, or a maximum amount of time spent on the phone (good luck with that one).

➤ Your child is going to take a while to learn how to budget, and will need your help. You can't just hand the money over and be done with it. To start with, make the allowances little and often. If you give your 15-year-old daughter a year's clothing allowance in April, she'll probably freeze next winter with no money left to buy anything warm. Give her a quarterly allowance and talk through with her what she thinks she'll need to buy. As she gets older you may be able to extend this to six-monthly or yearly. And maybe you can go shopping with her the first couple of times. An allowance for your child's cell phone might start off being monthly, and again you can talk through with your children how they'll make it last.

➤ If they run out of money through bad management and you bail them out, they'll learn nothing. So don't bail them out if you can possibly help it. If you have to, make sure it's something they won't want to happen again. For example, if your daughter is freezing come November and has no money left, buy her a cheap, clean, serviceable but not very fashionable secondhand coat from a charity shop. She won't let that happen again.

If you want to give your children more than one allowance, they'll find it easier to receive them separately. A certain amount for clothing, a separate allowance for movies, and so on. Then they can look after each amount individually. As they get older you can make it a bit more challenging by giving them one big sum to divide up between these various expenses. They'll learn how to do this more readily because they're used to separate allowances, and should be able to allocate their money sensibly as a result.

You might want to continue with the pocket money and/or interest system and add an allowance on top as your child gets older.

Match Funds

I'm not sure if the discussion about matching funds belongs here or later on where we look at earning money, but I'm putting it here. It's about giving your children money, and works well for children old enough to earn but unable to earn enough to buy anything really big.

Suppose your child wants to buy an iPod or a mountain bike. He might be saving for years at his current rate, however hard he tries. Well, it's no bad thing to have to wait, but there are limits. Sometimes you would like to help but you don't feel it's good for the kids to get something for nothing. Or anyway you simply can't afford to buy it outright.

With the match funds option, you offer to go halves, but they have to earn their half. Whether they get a Saturday job or clean neighbors' cars, if they can earn 50 percent, you'll match it. This isn't a way of financing their weekly chocolate bar, but it's a good way to put those really big items within their reach if they're prepared to work for it.

123

Open a Real Bank Account

Lots of people open savings accounts for their children, which can be an excellent thing. But sooner or later your children are going to need their own bank accounts. Certainly once they leave home, but why not before?

If you're paying your teenager an allowance for clothing or anything else, why not encourage him to open a bank account to keep it in—one with a checkbook and a debit card, too? That way he can register for online banking and learn to monitor the account and check the statements (and cope with mountains of junk mail, of course).

Checking accounts for children under the age of 18 varies across the United States from bank to bank. Some simply don't want to take on that business because minors can't be held financially responsible. You may want to start with the place where you do your own banking and ask. Or you may check with credit unions.

As for a credit card, a child under 18 may be added to a parent's account as a secondary card holder. Or you can get a prepaid debit card, where the money is put in first. You can check with your bank, but bottom line is usually your child won't be allowed a credit card under the age of 18, and she won't be allowed an overdraft or loan unless it's guaranteed by an adult. So you don't have to worry about the kids getting into debt to the bank, because it isn't possible.

By the age of 18, your child will be allowed to apply for a credit card and you won't be able to stop her. So maybe it would be a good thing if the kids had a couple years of experience behind them of running a bank account with their own allowance money to help them stay out of debt later.

Money In, Money Out

Your children need to learn the principle of balancing income and expenditure. If you follow the general process described earlier in this chapter, starting with 50 cents a week for candy and culminating in their own bank account for managing their own allowances by the time they're about 16, they'll be pretty well there.

But there are other things you can do to help them learn this basic principle. From quite a young age you can give them a basic budget for Christmas or birthdays, for example. You can tell them how much you can afford to spend on them, and they can decide whether to ask for an iPod or four Lego sets, because they're not getting both, though they might be able to have a cheaper iPod and one Lego set. Hmmm, it's their call.

Similarly, when they're small and you fund their buying Christmas presents for the family, you can give them a fixed budget and help them to stick to it. So if they get something a bit pricey for Grandma, they'll have to cut back when it comes to Uncle George.

You also need to make sure your teenagers know what they're *not* paying for. You wouldn't want them thinking that just because they can manage on their allowance now, that means they'll always be able to survive on that level of income. Talk to them about budgeting for rent (which is at least fairly pre-dictable), and electricity and phone bills (which may not be). As you've now taught them to think, as discussed in Chapter 4, "Teach Them to Think," you can get some lively discussions going on this topic if you time it right.

Food is the other big expense, along with general household goods. Okay, your son may not think that buying floor polish will be high on his priority list when he moves out, but he probably won't want to live the rest of his life without toilet paper or shampoo (well, just possibly the shampoo).

If you go shopping in the supermarket, get your teenager to come with you and give him a budget to stick to. It's a pretty tedious chore on a weekly basis, as we know only too well, but while it still has novelty value your teen will probably enjoy it and certainly learn a lot. Take a calculator, give him the budget and the shopping list you would have worked on yourself, and see if he can do any better. Maybe you could offer to split any savings he makes with him, to give him an extra incentive (though you may find yourself living on bread and water for a week).

Earning Money

It's all very well giving your children money, but that's not the real world, of course, not once they leave home. So it's a good idea to encourage them to earn some money of their own sooner or later.

Because the goal is to teach them how the adult world works, it's not in my view a good idea to pay them for doing jobs around the house that they should be doing anyway. For one thing, they will be hugely disappointed when they grow up to find that money doesn't fall into their bank account every time they do any house cleaning. For another thing, it undermines their attitude toward you as they get older: You do the laundry for nothing but they get paid for it. How fair is that? That just encourages them to take you for granted, and in the case of some children, particularly boys, it can teach them that it's a woman's job (if it's mom who usually does it), which men sometimes help with as a favor.

No, you're a family—a team—and you all pull together on group chores. You do more for them when they're little, and maybe later if they're working hard for exams or something, but essentially it's their job to help out in the house as much as it's yours. If you cook a meal, they ought to clear it up. If they wore the clothes, they should wash them. If you're doing more than your share it's a favor, and because you're not getting paid for it, nor should they. It's entirely up to you how many chores you expect your kids to help with, but whether it's few or many, they should be doing them for free.

That's not to say that your children shouldn't be able to earn money around the house, but it should be for doing *your* work for you, not chores they should be doing anyway. You can pay them to clean your workshop, or polish your shoes, or wash your car (though not for cleaning out the inside if it's their mess). It's entirely up to you and them what you pay them, but you need to be very clear what you expect for the money, and be sure they meet the standard that was agreed upon. Are they going to clean the car wheels? Wax or just soap and water?

Your children can earn money from other people, too. They may need some help from you finding work, and that's fine as long as they help and don't leave it all to you. They can dog walk, babysit, or wash cars for friends and neighbors. However, make sure they're not doing anything they're not equipped to do. You don't want your 10-year-old getting dragged into the road by an unruly Rottweiler, or your 12-year-old left responsible for an ill baby. So keep a close eye on the work they do.

Getting a Job

When your child reaches the age of 14, she can go into some kind of employment as long as the work does not interfere with the child's schooling, health, or well-being (in an agricultural situation that age can be as low as 12 with parental consent). There are limits on what a 14- to 16-year-old can do, such as jobs deemed hazardous, like mining, but there are plenty of jobs that are allowed. Once they reach 16, the options open up further. If you have any doubts, it's worth taking a peek at the Child Labor Laws, easily located on the Internet.

It's a good idea for your children to earn some kind of money for themselves before they leave home. It's not only about the money, it's the principle of having to turn up on time, be civil even if your boss drives you mad, get along with your fellow workers, and so on. And they learn about not only money in, money out, but also effort in, money out.

Saturday jobs and paper routes suit some children very well. However, not everyone is good in the mornings, and Saturday jobs do cut into free time and can be hard to come by. If your child really hates getting up, or gets a lot of homework at weekends, don't force her into a Saturday job. You really don't want her growing up learning that working is miserable and she never wants to do it if she can avoid it.

Summer vacation jobs are a much better alternative for many children. They can work hard for a few weeks of the year, without it interfering with school work or socializing time, and the hours over a year can easily add up to as much as a Saturday morning job.

If your children are earning money properly in this way, it will help to motivate them if you let them keep at least some of it to enjoy themselves with. If you tell them that now they're earning they can pay for their own clothes and you're stopping the clothing allowance, they'll wonder why they bothered. I know that's how life works when they're grown up, but they're not grown up yet, and they need breaking in gently. You can certainly reduce their clothing allowance by a proportion of what they earn, but make sure they have something left over for themselves after their hard work. They do deserve it.

Raising Money for Charity

There's one other way your children can learn about money by earning it, and that's through raising money for charity. This is a great way to encourage them to put effort in and get money out, and great to teach them to make the effort for other people and not always for themselves.

> Young people are often very ready to become ardent activists for a worthy cause, so harness this enthusiasm for making the world a better place, and do anything you can to help them raise money.

The very best causes are the ones where your child can see exactly where the money is going. Charities are getting better all the time at telling their supporters where the money goes. This doesn't mean you should discourage your child from donating to other charities, but try to steer him towards ones where he can see the effect.

129

For example, my children's elementary school once raised money for a school in Africa that had been almost demolished by a storm. The children were told that their fellow pupils in Africa had no roof over their heads, but that $10 would buy one sheet of corrugated roofing—60 sheets were needed to rebuild the school. The children could see that $10 each was an attainable target—60 students could roof the whole school.

This kind of clear reward for their hard work helps children understand money far better than dropping a coin into a collecting tin, and gives them a better sense of achievement, too.

It also helps to pick charities your child can identify with. Obviously children's charities are a favorite here, but so are animal charities, or those connected with any interests your child shares.

This is not just about encouraging your children to be altruistic, but also about helping them to understand money. You can talk to them about questioning how much of the money goes to administration, or why the marketing bill is so high, so they understand exactly where the money they have raised is going, and what it's achieving.

Get the Right Attitude

So you've taught your child how to manage their money and what they can buy with it. But that's not quite all you need to do. One of the most important things you can do for them is cultivate the right attitude toward money.

You know those people who can't get through a dinner party without asking you what your house is worth. Do you want your child to become one of them? Of course, you don't. Well, it's not just up to luck. You can help determine how your child views money.

The aim is that your kids see money as necessary for your family to keep out of poverty, and that anything more is a bonus. If you have more than enough it's great but it's not a big deal, and it's sensible to save what you can but not at the cost of become a stingy old miser. To encourage this attitude, there are certain things you need to do.

Don't Keep Going On About It

If you talk about money all the time, you'll give your child the clear impression that money is the most important thing in life. It isn't. There are so many things that are more important, most of them too saccharine to list here (friends, family—yuk, I can't go on, but you get my drift). If you don't often discuss money your kids will rightly see it as just another part of life.

Whether you're harping on about the fact that you can't afford this, and you can't afford that, or whether you're just endlessly discussing what things are worth (such as your house), you're giving out the wrong message.

Be Sensitive About People Who Have More or Less Money Than You

Your child needs to know that different people earn different salaries, and that it doesn't reflect on them personally. So never judge people in front of the kids (or, frankly, at all) on the basis of what they earn. That means not looking down on people who have less than you, but also not sounding jealous or resentful of people who earn more. ("Yes, well, they can afford it can't they?")

Your children need to learn not to assume that everyone else can afford what they can. If their friend's family has more disposable income than yours, that's really nice for the friend. End of story. If they have less, your child needs to see that you don't make a big deal of it. You don't smother them in pity (after all, money's not that important) but if your child complains that the friend won't come bicycling because he can't afford a decent bike, you point out gently that it's not his fault, and is there somebody who has a spare bike that could be used?

Show Them You Can Be Happy on a Budget

Have fun without spending a fortune. Don't let the only things that they enjoy be linked with spending or buying or generally high consumption. You don't have to say, "Look, we had fun on the cheap!" That suggests it's surprising, which it isn't. You just need your children to grow up knowing that happiness and money aren't linked, without having to tell them. If you get this right, it'll be obvious.

So, go out on some days to explore the countryside. Have vacations in the United States, and don't make it sound like a compromise because, "We can't afford a decent vacation this year." You're going to the seaside because it's as good a way as any to enjoy a week or two. To be honest, most of my very best vacations have been on nearby beaches. Yes, it's lovely going to exotic destinations if you can, because you'll learn a lot, but actually you couldn't possibly have a better time than you will building sandcastles, damming streams, and swimming in the sea anywhere in the United States. The company and the fun will count for so much more than the destination anyway.

I'm not saying you shouldn't spend money. I'm saying don't always spend money for the sake of it. If you can afford three weeks in the Bahamas, you can afford two weeks in the Bahamas plus one on a camp site along the Appalachian Trail. So do that instead. You'll get two vacations, and your kids will see that they were both as much fun as the other, without your having to labor the point—or even mention it at all.

Splurge Occasionally

If you're not doing the Bahamas thing, you can still splurge from time to time. Splurging for you might mean anything from a weekend in Orlando to a night out at the local pizza place. The point is that your children can see that although you're sensible with money, you're not tight-fisted. And why? Because as long as you have a roof over your heads and the bills are paid, money just isn't that important. If you never spend anything you don't have to, your children will be frustrated and could end up spending their own money like water as a reaction to a childhood where money was regarded as sacred and untouchable. In the end, if you can't enjoy it, what's it for?

Be Generous with Your Money

If you want generous-hearted children, you need to be gener-
ous yourself. Show them that it's a good way to be. I'm not
advocating throwing around money you don't have, or making a
big thing about it. I'm just saying that it's good for your kids to
see you put a bill rather than a coin in a collecting tin for a
charity you really believe in, or giving your partner an expensive
birthday present because you knew it was something she really wanted.

And, at least occasionally, buy your children a present when it's
not their birthday—just because you love them. If money is
tight, it only needs to be a funky hair barrette or a magazine
you spotted and knew they would really like. This small act just
reminds them that people are worth more than money, and
they, as your own children, are especially worth more. Yuk,
there I go again. Better stop now.

Money Sense

All children are different, and even if you do the very best to follow all the guidelines here, they won't all turn out exactly the
same. Some are inherently careful or insecure, and others
verge on the profligate. But if you do all you can to teach your
children to control their money while you're still there to keep
a steady hand, and you set them up with the right attitude to
the stuff, they will understand the value of money as well as
anyone.

Show Them That Broccoli Can Be Fun

We all want our children to live a long and healthy life. And the best way to do that is to bring them up assuming that a healthy lifestyle is a normal one. Of course, there are illnesses we and they have no control over, but there are also loads of conditions that are hugely more likely if your child grows up to be a fat, unhealthy couch potato.

The good news is that once *you* get into the habit of eating and acting healthily, it's very easy to get your child into the same habit. In fact it's almost inevitable. If you're not feeding your family as healthy a diet as you would like to, I don't deny it's an effort to change. However, it won't be an effort forever, though it may seem like it now. Habit is the critical thing about a healthy lifestyle, and once you've made the changes your new habit will become just as easy as your present one. I promise.

If you feel there's a lot to do to get your children's lifestyle as healthy as you would like, take it in stages. Set yourself a time-line—maybe decide to get their diet healthier by the end of May, and then spend the summer getting them into the habit of spending more time outdoors. Don't set yourself an impossible target, but do have a clear plan to keep yourself and the family on course.

Healthy Eating

At the absolute heart of healthy living is putting healthy food into our bodies. So the starting point here is to improve our children's diets. You can go and buy another book if you want to know exactly which vitamins and minerals are contained in which foods—that may well be useful but it's not what we're about here. You know perfectly well what foods are healthy without needing to be lectured about it: plenty of fresh fruit and vegetables, a good source of protein, minimal salt and refined sugars, not too much fat, and preferably not the saturated kind. If you stick to that, you can't go far wrong. So how are you going to achieve this goal relatively painlessly?

Don't Keep Unhealthy Food in the House

I know that not keeping unhealthy food in the house sounds obvious, but how many people do you know who do it? Certainly a few, but not very many. The fact is that if your child can't find a bag of potato chips or the Oreos, they're going to have to eat an apple and a piece of cheese instead. If you sometimes let yourself run out of bread, or you ration it, they can't make themselves a peanut butter and jelly sandwich and will have to eat a banana or a raw carrot instead. If there's no Coke, they'll have to drink juice or water.

Obviously, they'll moan and groan when you impose this new regime, but there will be nothing they can do about it. And within a very short time eating healthy will have become habit.

Unless your children are still too young to complain, there's no point thinking you can get away with this surreptitiously. You're going to have to be upfront about it. So here's what to do:

➤ Grit your teeth.

➤ Talk to the kids all at once (if you have more than one).

➤ Explain what you are doing and why. If you can find a way of telling them that it's for their own good without them wanting to hit you, congratulations. Use it.

➤ Tell them that you're not banning these foods totally—you're just not keeping them in the house. If they're not part of their normal diet, it will be fine to eat them at friends' houses, on vacation, or when they're out for a special treat.

➤ Think of an incentive to get them on your side—if everyone can stick to this for a month without complaining, there'll be a trip to the movies (popcorn included) at the end of it. Or whatever else suits you *except* don't reward them at the end of it with Twinkies or all the potato chips they can eat (more on this later). This just makes unhealthy food more desirable, and gives the message that you're imposing a regime of abstinence. You're not. You're simply replacing one regime with an even better one.

➤ Make sure there's always a fruit bowl on the table with plenty of enticing options, and any other healthy snacks your children will eat: unsalted nuts, carrot sticks and hummus, sticks of cheese to go with apples. (You don't want them stuffing themselves with cheese, but in moderation and as an accompaniment it's great.)

On the same principle, it's not a good idea for kids to grow up thinking that every meal should end with dessert. If this is what they've been used to, you need to change their habits so that dessert becomes an occasional thing, maybe when you have people over for a meal, or only with the Sunday roast. Otherwise they'll grow up expecting something sweet after every savory meal. Much better to push away your plate of risotto or steak or salad and feel you've finished a good meal, than always to feel there's still something missing.

> If your child wants to finish a meal with a piece of fruit, that, of course, is absolutely fine. What a great habit to get into, always grabbing an apple from the bowl after a meal.

Give Them Healthy Food with Variety

If you're anything like me, you'll know that there are few greater pleasures in life than good food. So why do our children think that macaroni and cheese, pizza, and spaghetti are the only things worth eating? I'm quite prepared to believe that your children are a lot broader in their tastes than some. But they're rarely as broad as we would like them to be.

Mostly what happens is that we start off giving them a pretty wide range of foods. But once they become toddlers, they start having opinions about it. After the third battle to get your child to eat spinach, it becomes so much easier just to stop cooking spinach. And the same goes for stir fries. Or rice. Or a banana. Slowly, without noticing, their repertoire diminishes. And the more children there are to please, the narrower becomes the range of foods that don't start arguments.

The thing to do is to make a concerted effort to get them to eat more variety. You have to do this consciously. Buy a couple of cookbooks or magazines, or get recipes from friends, or search for them online, and come up with ideas that you think might tempt your children. Serve your new ideas with vegetables or accompaniments that you know your children will eat, so if they refuse the main dish point blank at least they won't starve.

Look for ideas that will tempt them because they're fun. For example, if I serve my children chunks of cooked vegetables and then give them each their own bowl of cheese sauce to dip them in, like a fondue, they'll eat things I'd never get them eating otherwise. And I can always get them to eat beets because it turns their pee red, which is obviously truly exciting. Loads of friends will have other ideas, too.

And, listen, the thing is that it gets easier. Once your children stop expecting macaroni and cheese at least once a week, and instead expect something different on their plate every day, and often something they haven't seen before, they become more adventurous. They will try new things. Research shows that if you try anything enough times, you'll eventually like it (though my personal investigations have found this isn't true of raw celery).

I have one child who consistently refused things with "bits" in them. What he meant was anything that involved putting more than one foodstuff in his mouth at a time. Don't know why. This ruled out stir fries, risotto, chunky soups, loads of pasta dishes, and was generally a pain. So I started experimenting with soups that contained only top favorite foods of his: sweet corn, carrots, chicken, pasta stars. All chopped up large enough to identify but too small to pick out and eat individually. He ate these happily, and gradually lost his aversion to foods made up of "bits."

So, the moral is to encourage your children to enjoy experimenting with food. Here are some ideas:

➤ Unless you're vegetarian or vegan, aim to give them meat only three or four times a week at the most, and fish at least once, and to accept non-meat dishes as normal food the other days. After all they *are* normal food, and a diet that doesn't include meat at every meal is healthier than one that does.

➤ Actively look for new fruit and vegetables to try with your children. Don't give them carrots and sweet corn with every meal because you know they'll eat them.

➤ Go for as wide a range of colors on the plate as you can. Especially with fruit and vegetables, more color almost always means the kids are getting a wider range of nutrients, and they generally think it's more fun.

➤ Get your children to come up with ideas—maybe to come shopping with you—of new things they would like to try.

➤ Have fun presenting food in different ways that will appeal to your child. A teenager may not think it's funny to be given food carefully shaped into teddy bears, but he may well enjoy a chocolate "fondue" to dip his fruit into.

➤ If weekday meals are a frantic rush, start by experimenting just at weekends, and aim to vary weekday meals once your children are more open-minded, or with meals you've tested on them at weekends.

As you'll see in a minute, you should never force your children to eat anything they really don't like, but you can encourage them to try new things and praise them when they do, even if they decide not to eat the rest of it.

Set Up Healthy Patterns

The psychology of food is a huge and complex subject. But you know yourself that there's a strong relationship between your food and your emotions. From wanting comfort foods when you're ill to rewarding yourself with a chocolate bar at the end of a grueling day, the way we feel and what we eat are closely interlinked.

The same will be true for our children, all their lives. And it's pretty much entirely up to us what associations food has for them once they grow up. If we want them to eat healthily into adulthood, we need to make sure we don't set the wrong patterns. So here are a few of the most important things you can do.

> ➤ **Don't make them eat everything on the plate**—I know our parents and grandparents, especially if they were brought up during the war, made us do this. But it becomes a habit for life. What you end up with can be an overweight adult who has eaten more than enough and is no longer hungry, but still feels compelled to clear her plate, two or three times every day, seven days a week. That's a lot of unwanted and unneeded food piling on unhealthy pounds. The healthy thing to do is to stop eating once you're full.

> ➤ **Don't tell them they can't have dessert unless they eat their vegetables**—This translates as "healthy food is just the boring stuff you have to work through to get to the real fun." In other words, sweet, rich, fatty foods are where it's at.

> ➤ **Don't serve large portions**—Even without making your children eat everything on their plates, it's still much healthier to get them thinking that a modest

portion of food is what looks normal on the plate. After it's had five minutes to go down, and if they're still hungry, they can have a second helping. This method encourages them to eat only what they need.

➤ **Eat together at the table**—This makes healthy food the thing that brings the family together, and gives them a focus other than their food while they're eating. It's important to make dinnertime fun. It isn't the time to give everyone a hard time about not helping with the chores, or to nag about table manners. (Yes, it's the best time to point them out, but don't turn the dinner table into a battleground.)

➤ **Don't encourage them to eat unhealthy foods to excess**—You may have already removed all the candy, cookies, and potato chips from the house but other foods can be high in fat or cholesterol. Your children may not have a weight problem—now—but if they grow up always snacking on cheese and nuts they very well could later. So quietly run out of nuts, or switch to a cheese they like less, if you think they're developing habits they'll regret later.

➤ **Don't use sweet things as a reward or a bribe**—If you reward your children with a candy bar (or ice cream) now, you'll end up with adults who feel they "deserve" a Mars bar when they've had a productive day or reached a target. Well, obviously, most of us do deserve a Mars bar, but that doesn't mean we should expect to have one. By all means reward your children, just not with unhealthy food. If a carrot stick doesn't quite cut it, change tack and let them go to bed half an hour later or something.

➤ **Don't give them sweet food as a comfort**—Again, if you give your children a sweet snack because they've hurt themselves, they'll grow up to have irresistible urges to buy themselves chocolate when they're feeling depressed or low. (I can personally vouch for this.) If you're lucky they'll grow up to be slim, with naturally low cholesterol and they may get away with it. But they may not.

➤ **Don't ban treats altogether**—This is just as bad because it sets up sweet, fatty foods as some kind of ultimate, unattainable prize. Just keep them in moderation, and don't use them as rewards or comforters. There's nothing wrong with the occasional popcorn at the movies, or a packet of potato chips on a long car ride.

Don't Let Food Become an Issue

Everything I've covered so far should make "don't let food become an issue" a pretty predictable guideline. But it can be easier said than done. The trouble is that your children will know if they can get you wound up because they won't eat what you want them to, and even toddlers can be very manipulative if they know they have this control over you. Once this pattern starts, breaking it can be very difficult.

Be reassured that a young child won't starve himself. It just doesn't happen. I know older children can develop eating disorders, but one of the things you can do to prevent this is to make sure they grow up unaware that food can be a big deal to you. I know eating disorders are a far more complex thing than just this, but a laid-back attitude to eating will be a good starting point.

If you worry about what your children eat, watch them. If they're happy and healthy, and have plenty of energy, they must be getting the nutrition they need, even if you can't see where it's coming from. This is the bottom line. Always judge their diet by the end result, and if that's okay, don't fret.

If you're not fussing about them clearing their plate, and not forcing them to eat their vegetables, they'll end up pretty relaxed about food and they'll eat what they need, whatever age they are (barring eating disorders, for which you will obviously need to consult a specialist).

It's also worth mentioning that many children—and indeed many adults—can eat far more healthily if they eat five or six times a day. Little and often works much better for some children, especially while their stomachs are still small. And, of course, it keeps their blood sugar levels much more steady.

You can either give them three main meals but encourage them to have a healthy snack mid-morning and mid-afternoon, or you can increase the snack size and reduce the meal size until you have a balance that works well for them. This might be five very small meals a day, or three small meals and two good-sized snacks, or whatever does the trick.

Don't Let Them Become Overweight

According to surveys, parents often assess their children as being a healthy weight when they are in fact medically overweight to some degree. If your child becomes significantly overweight, you will have to do something about it, and this will generally result in

➤ Making an issue out of food
➤ Making them self-conscious about their weight
➤ Knocking their self-confidence

None of these are good things to inflict on your children, so the answer is to make sure they don't ever become overweight. And the way to do that is to nip any problem in the bud without their having to know about it. Don't kid yourself that this is just "baby fat." This is exactly the stage when a few simple adjustments can solve the problem.

So the moment you realize, if you're honest with yourself, that your child is starting to grow in the wrong direction, do something about it. If it really was just "baby fat," it won't matter. But if there was more to it than that, you should help get your child back into shape before it becomes a big challenge.

First of all, think about why your child is putting on weight. He must have changed his eating or exercising habits, so what's different? Has he started snacking on something more fattening? Does he now go to bed later and feel the need to fit in an extra snack? Has he started eating more at school? Or did he give up football at the end of last term? Or stop walking to school?

Once you've identified the problem, there are all sorts of subtle changes you can make to solve the problem before it gets out of hand. Here are just a few ideas, but you can be as creative as you like:

➤ Stop buying the fattening thing he's snacking on—
   full-fat yogurt, cheddar cheese, and so on—or
   replace it with a lower fat version.
➤ Serve the evening meal later so he doesn't need
   another snack before bed.

145

➤ Cut down on quantities at home if he's eating more at school.

➤ Encourage him to take up another sport, or take him bicycling on weekends.

➤ Reduce the time he spends in front of the TV. Change the house rules on the subject (more on this in a bit), or turn off the heating in the family room—you'll come up with something.

I know someone who noticed her son was putting on weight because he had started snacking in front of the TV in the evening. So she banned eating in the TV room, claiming it was because of the spills on the furniture. In the future he could eat only in the kitchen. She took the gamble that he would rather give up the snack than the TV, and she was right. Within three or four months his weight was back down to normal (she had caught the problem before his weight became a big issue) and he was none the wiser.

Remember that children are growing all the time, which gives you a big advantage. If you can just keep the amount of food they eat to a healthy level, those little areas of encroaching fat will get used up in the next growth spurt—but only if you make sure the calorie intake drops back, or the calorie expenditure goes up.

Teach Them to Cook

One of the very best things you can do for your children is to teach them to enjoy cooking. What better way for them to enjoy being healthy all their lives? There's no reason why a 10-year-old shouldn't be able to cook a family meal from time to time, even if it is usually a variation on a pasta bake; by their teens, the repertoire should be getting pretty interesting.

There are a few things to keep in mind here:

> ➤ All kids love baking, and, of course, they should be
> allowed to do it occasionally. But, actually, you don't
> want all those cakes and cookies in the house most
> of the time. Teach them to cook pasta or cauliflower
> and cheese sauce as well, and then move on to
> more varied meals.

> ➤ If you have more than one child, it is vastly easier to
> teach them to cook one-to-one. In this way, they
> become your assistant. So let them take turns with
> you rather than have a free-for-all.

> ➤ Make sure your child wants to cook the meal you're
> preparing together. As far as possible, let her
> choose what it will be.

It's pretty rare for children not to eat a good helping of a meal
they've chosen and cooked themselves, so not only are you setting up good habits for life, you're also making sure they get a
decent meal right now.

Keep Them Active

It's important for your children to be active for life, so as well as taking them to the park to play on the swings, you also want to breed enthusiasm for sports and activities that will keep them active all their lives. As with healthy eating, the idea is that they grow up assuming that plenty of physical activity is normal. That means they need to see you bicycling or playing tennis—or at the very least getting out of doors when the weather's nice.

Let Them Find Activities They Enjoy

If you force your children to do ballet, judo, or football, they'll give it up the second they get the chance, whether that's when they're eight or 18. And you'll have achieved nothing. The only way physical activity like this is going to work is if you let them choose what they want to do.

The thing is that they probably don't know themselves what to choose. They need to try a few things to see what really does it for them. Too many parents tell their child, "You said you wanted to go to Brownies/learn karate/do swimming. So now I've sorted out the lessons/bought you the kit/found a teacher, so you can forget about quitting."

Actually, that's not fair. They couldn't know they weren't going to like it. Have you never gone to a party you thought you would enjoy and then left early because it was so dull? Or started a great-sounding job and then found you hated it? It's better really to view your child starting any new activity as a taster to see whether she enjoys it. And don't buy the gear until the child has been doing it for a while.

Don't make them do anything they hate, but keep looking until you find something they love. I've never met a child who didn't have anything he enjoyed, if both the child and parents looked hard enough. Often it's easy, because the kids are football fanatics or dedicated tennis players. Sometimes you need to find something less obvious to tempt them. Depending on money and resources, lots of children get really fired up about activities such as horseback riding, surfing, tae kwon do, diving, gymnastics, soccer, sailing, or snowboarding.

> You know your child. You probably know whether she hates team sports or loves being out of doors. Look for the kind of activities that suit your child and, sooner or later, you'll find something.

Get Kids to Walk or Bike to School

When I was young, almost everyone walked to school. Or they walked to and from the bus stop if they lived further away. Nowadays, almost everyone seems to drive their kids to school. For a few people there's no choice, but most times there is.

It's just that we can get a little too overprotective. We worry what might happen to them if they're on their own. Actually, the answer is to give them the skills they need to be safe. The odds of your child's being abducted in broad daylight at school are a lot lower than the odds on your having a serious car accident driving him to school. And if you've taught your children road safety, they need to practice it on their own. I know it's worrying, but that's what being a parent is all about.

If you need to drive them, why not drop them off a mile or so from the school gates? Do you really have to take them to the door? The reason they're going there is to learn, so let them learn some independence, too, on their way there.

It makes such a difference to your child's health to walk a mile or two routinely every day. But more than that, it sets another pattern for life. When they're grown up, it will be far healthier to park in the parking lot and walk around to the stores, rather than to drive up and down the street looking for spaces to park outside every shop in order to save walking. That's what unfit grown-ups do. And that's not what we want our children to do. We want them to regard it as natural to walk for 15 or 20 minutes to reach where they're going to, not to arrive at the door by car.

Arrange Exercise by Stealth

Not all exercise needs to be labeled as such—walking to school is one example—where exercise serves a purpose, but there are plenty of other ways you can get your child active without it being a sport or activity. Take your children out into the countryside or the nearest park and see who can reach the top of the hill the fastest. Or go into the woods to see whether you can find any toadstools, or squirrels, or whatever—it doesn't have to be "going for a walk." Borrow a neighbor's dog and get the kids to help you take the dog out. Find one of those parks with an interesting bicycle track or an adventure playground or a skateboard course. Buy your child a skateboard on eBay, or a scooter. If it sounds intriguing and fun, then kids are unlikely to realize it is exercise, however much they might resist it usually.

Ration Screen Time

We're always being told that our children spend too much time in front of the TV or computer screen, to the detriment of their health. And it's true. Every hour your child is in front of a screen is an hour wasted when she could have been getting exercise, even if it's just running around the house with a brother or sister, or out in the garden playing with the hose. It doesn't necessarily have to be any kind of organized sport, just some kind of physical activity.

To achieve this level of activity, there are only two things you need to do:

> ➤ Ration time spent in front of a screen (Game Boy, Xbox, TV, PC, or whatever)
> ➤ Don't let your kids have a PC or TV in their room

If you remove these activities for most of the time, your child will choose to do something more active. Occasionally, of course, they'll choose to sit and do a jigsaw puzzle or build a model dinosaur. Many parents would prefer those to TV time. Most of the time, though, the child will be moving around at least.

A couple hours of screen time a day (altogether) should be ample for any child on a day he is not at school. On school days aim to have at least two or three hours of free time at home. So if your kids get home three hours before they go to bed, don't allow screen time on school days. As they get older and bedtime gets later, you can allow it after, say, 7 p.m. or 8 p.m., if all their homework is done.

Once your children reach mid-teens, controlling how they spend their time gets virtually impossible. And, indeed, they need to learn to manage it for themselves. But if you've kept screen time down to a sensible level right up to the age of about 15, it won't matter so much. They may binge on TV for a couple of years, but as adults they'll revert to a more balanced approach. And why? Because during the first 15 years of their life they learned how to occupy themselves without needing a moving picture on a screen to do it for them.

Every so often, my children have gotten into the habit of watching too much TV. Invariably this is because one or more of them has been ill and the rules have been relaxed. I remember a six-week spell during all of which at least one of them was ill with chickenpox. When we reverted to rationed screen time at the end of it, they had all forgotten how to play by themselves. They spent a couple of days wandering round saying, "I'm bored" and squabbling with each other. After a few days, though, they went back to finding their own amusements and inventing their own games. It just shows what permanent damage TV and computers must do to children's minds.

If your children are young enough, you can resist any call ever to put a screen in their room. If it's already there, I realize things will be trickier. Ration their time and then tell them that if they prove they can be trusted to stick to it with the screen in their room it can stay, but if you catch them "cheating" you'll remove the screen.

Healthy Mind

As well as a healthy body, you also want your children to grow up with healthy minds. So how are you going to make sure that happens? Well, making sure they have a good attitude about their body is a good place to start.

Encourage Them to Have a Good Body Image

Having a good body image applies to both boys and girls. It's important that they don't grow up thinking that they can only be happy if their butt is smaller or their acne clears up. This kind of thing can dominate some people's view of themselves, and cause adults to feel insecure and under-confident for life. It can have an impact on their relationships and, crucially—as with so many things—the way they raise their own children. So you need to get this part right for your grandchildren's sake, too.

➤ **Make only positive comments**—The first thing is to make sure that the only comments you ever make on their appearance are positive ones. Never criticize the way they look, from the shape of their nose to the size of their stomach.

➤ **Make sure they won't have trouble living up to your comments in future**—If you comment on the color of their hair or eyes, or how cheerful their smile is, that's fine. But if you tell them how lucky they are to be so naturally slim, how will they feel in 20 years' time when they've put on 40 pounds?

➤ **Don't let them develop a weight problem**—We've already looked at this; make sure you deal with any

153

potentially unhealthy increase in weight before it needs to be mentioned to them.

➤ **Don't let them see or hear you speaking negatively about your own body**—It's no good being positive about your child but constantly moaning about your own beer belly or bags under your eyes. Not only does it tell them that conforming to stereotype body images is important, but also there's a good chance that they'll inherit your beer gut or your bags. If you moan that you're fat, and 20 years later they end up with your body shape, it's going to sound pretty hollow when you tell them how great they look.

➤ **Don't make a big issue out of the way you look**—Of course, looks count for more than perhaps they should. People do judge by appearances. But as long as your children know how to look presentable when they need to, there's no point making them think that the way they look should influence how happy they are. It shouldn't, but it will if you let them think it should.

➤ **Don't keep dieting in front of them**—Again, this just tells them that they can't be happy unless they're thin. Even if this is true for you, all the more reason not to inflict the same mindset on your child. If you really must diet (and if you're following a healthy eating plan with the family doing so shouldn't really be necessary), then no fad diets. Just cut down in such a way that your kids don't notice you're dieting. And don't mention it to them.

➤ **Don't criticize other people's appearance**—If you don't want your children to think that they'll be judged on their appearance don't get caught making the same mistake yourself. No saying, "She's let herself go," or "Have you seen how much weight he's put on?" or "Poor guy, bald at the age of 30."

Help Them Deal with Their Own Emotional Baggage

In order to be healthy emotionally as well as physically, your children will need to learn how to face up to their own shortcomings. Whether they are prone to depression, anger, worry, or any other negative outlook, they'll need to learn to cope. That means that you need to help them find strategies to deal with it. You may be lucky and have an easygoing child with no such problems. But I bet that if you have more than one child, at least one of them will have her own inner demon. Most of us do.

I can't tell you what the strategies are—it depends on your child. But you need to talk to her, pass on any experience of your own, ask other people how they cope with the same things, and explore solutions through the Internet, books, or whatever else works for you.

Some children can usefully be taught meditation at an early age; others get a lot of benefit from music. Every child is different. But if yours is prone to outbursts of anger, help him discover an outlet for it, whether it's going for a run, learning the drums, or punching a pillow. Teach your negative-minded child to recognize the onset of a bout of negativity or depression and go for a walk, or spend time with other people instead of alone in his room, or sing—whatever does it for him. Show your anxious child how to use yoga breathing, or to talk through her worries, or to distract herself.

Show Them How to Manage Stress

Few of us go through life without ever getting stressed. And there's no way you can prevent it happening to your children. But you can make sure that when they get stressed, you show them how to deal with it. I realize that they don't always take kindly to this advice at moments of high stress, so you may have to pick your words carefully, or wait until they've recovered and then make suggestions for next time (to be used, preferably, before you're in range).

Again, different techniques work for different people, but here are some ideas:

> ➤ To start with, if your child recognizes the cause of the stress, he needs to consider whether it's avoidable. If he regularly gets stressed by having a bad day at school because he arrived late, he needs to spot the clue: Get up earlier and life will be easier.

> ➤ Meditation and yoga work very well for some children (and not for others).

> ➤ Listening to music can be effective, or playing an instrument.

> ➤ Physical activity of some kind is a great stress reliever. Help your child to discover what kind of activity helps her best: running, walking, cycling, hitting a punching bag....

> ➤ Some people feel better if they talk it out with someone; others find this just gets them more wound up.

> ➤ Being alone with some kind of distraction, or a warm bath, might be a good solution.

Ideally, your child needs a range of techniques. As an adult, it's not always going to be possible to jump into a warm bath whenever she feels stressed, so she needs fast solutions, too, whether that's running, counting to ten, or yoga breathing.

Make sure your child understands that, while you're sympathetic to the stress, it is not acceptable to take it out on other people. Let your kids know, and see, that you withdraw the sympathy if they do this. It's a habit that all children adopt but it won't get them very far in adult life and it's your job to show them that it's the wrong way to deal with stress.

Set Up for Life

Much of our health as an adult is dependent on the patterns of thinking and behaving that were set when we were children. That's why the way you teach your child to view food, exercise, and mental well-being will have such a huge impact on how happy and healthy they become as adults. It's a big responsibility, and few people get it spot on every time, but it's perfectly possible to get this right, and it really is one of the most important things you can do for your children.

Give Them Each Other

I firmly believe that if you have more than one child, the absolute most important thing you can possibly do is to make sure that they have a really strong bond with each other for life. However good your friends are, family is better. When you go through the real crises in life—divorce, bereavement, the big stuff—it's your family you want beside you. And if things go right, it's your family who you want to be there, dropping everything and flying halfway round the globe if need be.

Okay, so you would always drop everything for your kids. But are you sure you're going to be able to do that if they're widowed at the age of 70? Will you really be there when their grandchild is terrifyingly ill? No, probably not. But there's a good chance their siblings will be around for most of it. And who else is going to understand exactly what they're going through when it's finally your turn to shrug off the mortal coil?

In other words, they're almost certainly going to have each other for a great deal longer than they're going to have you. So you need to lay the foundations now for a really strong, close, understanding, supportive bond that will last all their lives. Can you think of anything more worthwhile that you could give them?

Of course, when they're busy scratching each other's eyes out over whose turn it is to have the free gift out of the cereal box, it can seem quite hard to imagine how you're ever going to achieve this. But don't worry—squabbling, if you handle it right, is all part of the bonding process. I discuss that later.

> Meanwhile, there are a few basic ground rules that can help ensure that your children grow up loving one another rather than hating each other (though, of course, it won't be cool to admit it).

I should just add that if you have only one child, family bonds really are stronger than friendships. Most of us can tell you far more about what our cousins are up to than we can about the person who was our best friend all through elementary school. So try to keep your child as closely in touch as possible with family of his own age, to give him the closest thing he can have to a sibling relationship.

Treat Them Differently (Without Being Unfair)

Your children are all different people. They have different likes and dislikes, different strengths and weaknesses, different innate skills, and different reactions. If you had a pet camel and a pet bird, you wouldn't expect to treat them the same. (Personally, I would start by selling the camel.) I've known siblings who were more different than camels and birds.

But there is a prevailing view that it isn't fair to treat your children differently. Well, would it be fair to treat a camel and a bird the same? I suppose you could find some midpoint that would just about do for both of them (can't quite think what that would entail) but actually that would be unfair to both of them.

> The challenge with kids is to treat them differently because they're different people, but not to be unfair. And that can be tricky. After all, kids are generally pretty swift to spot any discrepancy (unless it's in their favor).

Let's take an example to illustrate the problem. Child A is really good at doing the dishes. In fact, he quite enjoys it and can do it efficiently and easily. When it's Child B's turn, she spends hours at the sink in tears because she hates it so much that it seems like an overwhelming task.

Now, if you were to let Child B off ever doing the dishes, that would indeed be unfair, and Child A would be justified in complaining. On the other hand, if you insist that they take it strictly in turns to do it equally, that's actually unfair to Child B. Why? Because you're asking far more of her than you are of Child A.

And that's the crucial thing. You should expect the same *effort* from each of your children, but this won't necessarily translate into the same results. So perhaps Child B doesn't have to do the dishes up quite so often. Or maybe she gets helped more. Whatever you think best—they're your children. Of course, by the time Child B is 18, you'll be expecting her to take her turn doing the dishes as often as A. But you'll have weaned her there a bit more gently.

Meanwhile, lest this still seems horribly unbalanced to you, I should tell you that Child A is dreadful at getting up in the mornings for school, while Child B is always dressed and has eaten breakfast before the rest of the house is awake. Child B is expected to set the table for breakfast, open the curtains, and let the dog out in the mornings, while Child A has no morning chores at all. Is this fair? Of course it is, because it's far more effort for A to drag himself downstairs and out of the door than it is for B to do all her chores. Mind you, A has chores after school, by which time he's usually just about awake.

You see, the thing is that you'll create resentment if you try to make all your children conform to some kind of norm—resentment of you and of each other, for pushing up the standard to a point their sibling can't hope to attain. Whereas if you set the standard for effort rather than for achievement, they can all get there at their own pace. If they question it, you can point out that it's perfectly fair on those terms. And no doubt you can also point out to the child who is questioning you where this system is working in her favor.

Never Compare Them with Each Other

We touched on not making comparisons between siblings in Chapter 7, "Make Sure You See the Forest *and* the Trees." You will certainly create rivalry if you tell one child that she is better, slower, brighter, worse-tempered, stronger, kinder, funnier, or anything else than her brother or sister.

It can be hugely tempting to say, "Why can't you just do your homework without a fuss, like your sister does?" Or, "Your brother could swim when he was half your age." A child is bound to resent the sibling who has set the bar so high and won your approval where she has failed.

It simply isn't relevant what her sibling does or doesn't do. If all your children were exactly the same, what would be the point of having more than one child? It's not actually helpful to compare them with anyone, whether it's "Your friend Sam can do her shoelaces up by herself," or "I read a survey last week that said 90 percent of 12-year-olds clean their rooms at least once a week. So why can't you?" But what we're concerned with here is sibling relationships, and the very worst sin of comparison you can commit is to compare your child with her brother or sister.

Play No Favorites

Some parents are lucky. They really, genuinely, truly don't have a favorite child. Many parents do, though. You know you shouldn't, you feel guilty about it, but there it is—you just prefer one to another.

Of course, the problem here is that favoritism tends to show, however hard you try to hide it, and is a surefire way to create real long-term trouble between siblings.

The first and most important thing is that you must never let it show. If necessary, overcompensate slightly in order to conceal the fact. There's no point going into denial about it to yourself—if you do that you won't be able to deal with it—but never discuss it with anyone else, except possibly your partner. There's always the danger someone will blab, if only by mistake, or share the information in a less-than-sober moment with an unreliable friend.

The next thing to do is to think about whether it's really true. I know one father who says that he actually loves all his children equally. But sometimes he likes one best. He adds that it isn't always the same one; in fact, most of them have been favorite at some time. What he really means by this is that he sometimes enjoys one child's company more than another's. Well, that's inevitable up to a point. But it doesn't mean you don't love them equally, as he recognizes.

Suppose, however, that you really do believe that you love one child less than the other. What can you do about it? Here are some thoughts that may help you:

➤ We often find it easier to relate to a child who is similar to us. If one child takes after the other parent, and you don't really get what makes her tick, that can make it harder to feel a strong bond. So talk to your partner or whomever the child takes after and find out more about how this person thinks and feels.

➤ Sometimes you dislike certain traits in your child, often because he takes after your ex, or the mother you always had a tricky relationship with, or perhaps even yourself. So consciously note all the traits you *do* appreciate in this child, and try to focus on those.

➤ Look for all the characteristics your child has that are similar to you (and that you don't dislike). Your child is composed of 50 percent you, after all, so there must be something. Maybe you both love music, or like spending time alone, or worry about little things. Again, focus on the similarities so that your child doesn't seem so alien.

➤ Try to spend time, just the two of you, doing things that you have in common—cooking, going to the movies, being out of doors. If you can strengthen the relationship like this, you can often resolve the problem.

➤ One thing that can easily happen, especially in families with two parents and two kids, is that you split into pairs. And often each child hangs out with the parent she gets along best with. Actually, this is great some of the time, but if it's a regular thing it just makes the problem worse. Try to spend more time with the less favored child. Just building a closeness and a bond will often remove the favoritism.

➤ Sometimes one child is less favored because she makes your life difficult. It seems impossible to love your rude, ill-tempered, teenage daughter as much as your cute, nine-year-old little boy. In this case, try to find ways of spending time with your teenager that you'll both enjoy and won't create flashpoints. What does she enjoy? Could you treat her to a trip to a fashion show? If you're not trying to make her clean her room, get off the phone, do her home-work, and so on, there's less to argue about and you may get to see the lovable side of her more often.

Dealing with Squabbles

Unless you have a pretty substantial age gap, you can't have more than one child without having squabbles. Actually, how-ever, while some children fight because they hate each other, the majority fight despite the fact that they love each other. Most of the closest adult siblings I know insist that they fought endlessly as children. So the fact your kids fight with each other may drive you to distraction, but it doesn't indicate that they won't grow up to have the relationship you want for them—far from it.

The fact is that sibling squabbles are healthy. And infuriating, frustrating, exasperating, and exhausting...for you. But for your kids, healthy. Once they have grown up, your children will need to be able to get along with colleagues, bosses, friends, acquaintances, mechanics, shopkeepers, neighbors, tutors, customers, public officials, fellow parents—and all the rest of them. Some of these people will be delightful, but a few will be downright difficult. And some will be lovely people most of the time but very stressed right now. How are you going to train your child to cope with all these people?

You aren't, actually. Because if you have more than one child, their siblings will train them for you. The downside of this arrangement is that, although you're largely off the hook (not completely, as you'll see), their siblings have a rather noisy and confrontational style of training. Still, it's their job, and they have to do it their way.

The thing is, sibling squabbles are the safe way to learn what people will and won't put up with, and what tactics do and don't persuade people to change their minds, and how to elicit cooperation from people. If you have more than two children it gets even better, because they learn instinctively that what works with one person doesn't necessarily work with another.

If one pushes it too far with a classmate at school, he can tell you, "I'm not your friend any more!" But a poor old sibling doesn't have the option of saying, "I'm not your sister any more!" She is stuck with you. Which is why, as a child, you can go on practicing your interpersonal skills on her for 18 years and she can't stop you. She can practice back, though.

Teach Them to Sort Out Their Own Arguments

So far, so good. But I did say you weren't entirely off the hook, and this is because your children need to learn how to resolve squabbles; otherwise, at the age of 18 they'll still only know how to shout, "It's mine!" "No, it's not, it's mine!" They'll learn some problem resolution skills by themselves, but they'll need a bit of help from you, too.

They'll learn nothing if every time when they squabble you wade in and sort everything out. "Right, that's it. Sam, you can watch this program for half an hour. And then Matt, you can change the channel and watch your program." No, you have to be smarter than that.

The first rule is not to intervene at all unless things start to turn nasty. Just stop and listen to them—it's always fascinating to see which of your kids is the diplomat, which is the most manipulative, which relies on threats, and which one cajoles. So leave them alone to sort things out whenever you can. As they get older, they'll be able to do this more and more often, especially if you're intervening the right way when you do have to butt in.

The trick to intervening is not to solve the problem yourself—that's their job. You just give them a very good reason to solve it. And you do that by removing the focus of the squabble—literally or figuratively—and refusing to return it until they have a solution. In other words, you take away the toy, turn off the TV, ban all breakfast cereals, or decree that no one is allowed to sit in the front of the car—until they collectively come to you with a solution they've all agreed upon. If they can't agree, no one gets the toy, the TV, the free gift, or the front seat.

When they're little, you'll probably have to give them a few clues. You'll need to suggest some solutions to choose between; for example, "You could play with it together, or you could take it in turns, or you could let him play with it if he lets you play with a special toy of his." As they get older, not only will this rarely be necessary, but they'll also come up with creative solutions that will sometimes amaze you.

For your part, you have to accept their solution unless you've a very good reason not to. If you privately think it won't work, well, let them find that out for themselves.

She Started It!

The other kind of squabble is the one where they're not actually arguing over a toy or access to the TV or anything like that. The first you know of it, they're flinging accusations back and forth about who snatched what from whom, and who kicked who.

> Don't get caught up in these arguments, whatever you do. You will never get to the bottom of it, and I can tell you anyway that they're both in the wrong.
> And I wasn't even there.

I only know one way to deal with this kind of argument, and that is to get them both to confess their sins. (However many kids you have, these are usually one-to-one combats.) On no account should you ask a third sibling to intervene on behalf of one of them, because this is obviously asking for trouble. That's the kind of divide-and-conquer tactic employed by parents whose children grow up to hate each other.

How on earth do you get them to confess? Well, it's surprisingly easy. Once they get the hang of the system, they appreciate it because it means the other one confesses, too, which gives them justice of a kind. With boys, you can generally propose an "honesty competition." They're so competitive they can't resist anything dressed up that way. Some girls will fall for this method, too, but if not you can always offer some kind of "carrot and stick" as you might call it (as you saw in Chapter 1, "Make Their World Solid"). You can't actually reward them with a prize because that will encourage them to do it again. But you can offer to not punish them: "If you tell me honestly what you did, I won't cancel your TV time tonight." As I said, you may not even have to do that.

My children are very used to this ploy. It goes like this:

Parent:	Let's take it in turns, and see who can be most honest. Now (to first child), what did you do that you shouldn't have done?
First child:	I snatched a toy from him and hit him on the arm.
Parent:	Thank you for being honest. Now (to second child), what did *you* do that you shouldn't have done?
Second child:	I punched her in the stomach and called her stupid.
Parent:	Thank you. And (to both) what do we say to people when we've hurt or upset them?
Both children	(to each other): Sorry.
Parent:	Well done for being honest. Now off you go.

There is a rule you have to have, which is that you *only* say what it was you did wrong, and never why. Your child isn't allowed to say, "I snatched it *because she wouldn't give it back.*" Or, "*After he punched me,* I hit him." If they try to do this, gently but firmly stop them and remind them it's not allowed.

I have to say I have one child who is so honest (or should that be so competitive?) that he invariably asks for 17 other offenses to be taken into consideration.

I sometimes wonder why this works, but I have never known it to fail. Well actually, I think I do know why it works. It's because it's worth confessing for the payoff of hearing the other one admit honestly what she did to you. The kids always go back to playing together quite happily afterwards. And curiously, none of them has ever asked me who won the honesty competition.

Create a Sense of Unity

As well as these tactics are designed to prevent unnecessary enmity between your children, there are also plenty of techniques for actively bringing them closer together. These are all things you can do over the whole 18 years you're in charge, so that over time they develop a sense of being a strong unit, albeit one that sometimes has its internal frictions.

Encourage Them to Play Together

You'll no doubt have noticed that parents of only children become their child's chief companion, especially for the first half of their childhood. If you have more than one child, you can step back and encourage them to play together. Of course, you can step in sometimes for a treat (to yourself) when they're tired and crotchety, or one of them really wants to play alone. The aim is that on balance your children grow up seeing one another as their primary companion. That sort of bond lasts right through their lives.

Encourage Them to Support Each Other

When your child asks for help with their homework, or getting the DVD player to work, or mending a broken toy, there's no need to do it yourself every time. It's far better for your children to grow up regarding it as normal to help each other out. Of course there'll be resentment if you forever make one of them drop what he's doing in order to sort out something for his brother and sister. But as long as you don't overuse this tactic, it's very effective. Your other child will be flattered if you say, "I'm hopeless with technology, but I bet Tilly can help you," or "Math isn't really my thing. Try asking Charlie."

It's great if you can find ways in which younger siblings can help older ones. Anything that irons out the hierarchy is a good thing, because once they're grown up it won't be helpful. They'll want to see each other as equals. Okay, so your younger child might struggle with his older sister's math homework, but he can still fetch a pair of socks from her wardrobe on the way downstairs, or help look for her escaped gerbil.

Exploit Each Child's Strengths

Hand in hand with supporting each other, having your children recognize each other's strengths is always a good thing. Maybe one of your children is especially good at remembering things ("Don't let me forget to buy butter when we get to the shop; I forgot to write it on the list"), or finds it really easy to organize things. Some children can always find anything that's gone missing ("Sam, have you seen where I put my keys down? You're good at noticing where things are"), or is a particularly good cook, or can always think of something to keep everyone cheerful on long journeys.

With your help, they'll soon be asking each other, "Can you remind me when we get to school to hand in my homework?" or "Hey, Sam, any idea what I did with my iPod?" It's important here not to overlook a child with the same talent. If you always ask Charlie to help you find things, Tilly will feel slighted if she reckons she knows where things are, too. But if she's as hopeless as you, she'll really appreciate Charlie's help in finding things.

Put Each Child in Charge of Different Tasks

This is a good way to help your children recognize each other's strengths. You can give children their own regular tasks, which also helps to give them a sense of responsibility and pride in what they do. So, for example, one child can be in charge of putting things down on the shopping list, or keeping the DVDs in order. That means that her siblings will have to refer to her if they want to be sure you buy more cornflakes, or they can't find the DVD they left in the machine last weekend.

A word of advice here: You can put children in charge of tasks, but it's rash to put them in charge of each other. It's fine for Tilly to decide how to organize the DVDs, but she shouldn't have the authority to ban her brother from watching his favorite movie as a punishment for not putting it away properly last time. She'll need to refer any disciplinary matters to you.

Don't Let Your Children Tell Tales

If one of your children steals another one's toy, it's not unreasonable for the victim to complain to you. Indeed, that may be preferable to taking the matter into his own hands. Tattle telling is when one child complains about something the other has done *that doesn't affect them personally*. So, if Charlie tells you that when you were in the bath, Tilly spent an hour on the phone, that's tattling. The only point of telling you is to get Tilly into trouble, and actually you want your children to stick together.

The thing to do in this case is to make sure that the child who tells tales comes off worst. You might say, "Tilly shouldn't have done that," but the focus is on, "but you shouldn't be telling tales on her. It's not kind to try to get your sister into trouble." Once the child realizes he's the one who gets told off when he tells tales, he'll soon stop.

Talk to Your Children Collectively

The more you treat your children as a team unit, the more they'll behave like one. So get them together as a group as often as you can. Family mealtimes are a great time to do this, and it's one of many reasons why it's worth making the effort to eat together. As the children get older this becomes increasingly difficult, but even if you can make it only once or twice a week, it's an important part of bonding your children together.

For some families, the ride to school is the next best time to get together, but it usually means only one parent is there.

> Once you have all your children together, this is the time to share information with them. It's a bit like a team briefing, really. Let them know what's happening this weekend, discuss jointly where to spend Christmas this year, or agree on whose turn it is to cook Sunday lunch.

It's also a good idea to pass on any instructions or training to your children when they're all together. It all adds to that sense of unity, and it means you should have to say it only once. (After that they can remind each other to save you repeating yourself.) So if you want to tell them your cunning plan for making them earn their pocket money, or explain that the new shower won't work unless they turn on the switch first, or run through how to use the timer on the VCR, assemble the children first. (Yes, obviously I meant *they'll* be showing *you* how to use the timer on the VCR.)

Give Group Rewards for Group Achievements

If your children have worked together for something that warrants a reward, make sure you reward them as a team. Suppose they've all taken it in turns to cook supper while you've had that dreadful flu bug, or everyone worked hard to clear the kitchen ready for redecorating. In that case, treat them as a team and take them all out to the fair together, or let them stay up together to watch a movie that's on TV late.

All for One, One for All

War is known for its ability to bond people together during adversity. All families have crises from time to time, whether because of some tragedy such as illness, or whether it's some kind of natural disaster—the car's broken down 50 miles from home, or the roof's blown off the kitchen.

If you can keep everyone's spirits up, there's a huge sense of achievement in working together to overcome these problems. Maybe it's a case of everyone working outdoors in a thunderstorm clearing drains and gutters before the hall floods, or perhaps everyone chips in with the household chores while one of you looks after the sick grandmother. Whatever the challenge, your children will learn very fast to recognize each other's value in these situations, especially if you can gently guide each of them towards tasks they're good at, if necessary, so everyone is seen to have contributed.

Once the drains are clear, and the rain is safely diverted away from the house, you can wrap them all in blankets and make them cocoa, while they each relive their dramatic account of the crisis. If that doesn't help forge a bond for life, nothing will.

Conclusion

We all want our children to grow up to be happy, successful in their own terms, loved by others, and able to cope with life. There are lots of things we can do as parents to achieve this, and this book sets out the 10 most important of all. Get these 10 tools right, and the rest will follow.

Raising children is a long, hard struggle. But then nothing worth having comes for nothing, and the work can be as much fun as the end result (well, not all of it, but a lot of it). If you can stay focused on what really matters, and not get bogged down in the details of odd socks, spilled drinks, and messy bedrooms, you'll find after 18 years that you've not only produced children you can be proud of, but also wonderful people whom you will find yourself loving happily and unconditionally for the rest of your life. Now that has to be worth any effort.

Index

in small steps, 98-99
techniques for, 101-102
sleepovers, children's responsibility during, 44
space, providing for imaginative play, 24-28
specialness, telling children of, 17-18
sports
  letting children choose, 148-149
  number to enroll in, 25-26
spouses. *See* parents
squabbles among children, handling, 166-171
status, as motivation, 73
"sticks." *See* punishment
strengths
  differences from parents', handling, 68, 70
  encouraging among siblings, 172-174
  insecurities, overcoming, 74-81
  motivations, determining, 72-74
  praise for, 11, 15-18
  role in teaching skills, 109
  world views, respecting, 70-71
stress management, teaching, 156-157

supporting each other (siblings), 172
swimming lessons, importance of, 26

T

talking with children
  about overcoming insecurities, 78-81
  about responsibilities, 46-47
  instilling values by, 42-43
tattle telling, discouraging, 174
teaching skills
  avoiding comparing children, 103-104
  beginning early rather than late, 101, 115-116
  children's personalities, role of, 109
  cleaning children's rooms, 105-108
  emotional skills, 113-115
  keeping track of progress, 100
  list of essential skills, 110-113
  reminding children, 104-105
  in small steps, 98-99
  techniques for, 101-102
team, treating siblings as, 174-175

W

FT Press

FINANCIAL TIMES

In an increasingly competitive world, it is quality
of thinking that gives an edge—an idea that opens new
doors, a technique that solves a problem, or an insight
that simply helps make sense of it all.

We work with leading authors in the various arenas
of business and finance to bring cutting-edge thinking
and best-learning practices to a global market.

It is our goal to create world-class print publications
and electronic products that give readers
knowledge and understanding that can then be
applied, whether studying or at work.

To find out more about our business
products, you can visit us at www.ftpress.com.